KNUTSFORD I
THE INSIDE S

KNUTSFORD PRISON
The Inside Story

DAVID WOODLEY

AN IMPRINT OF
ANNE LOADER
PUBLICATIONS

ISBN10: 1 901253 27 9
ISBN13: 978-1-901253-27-6

Published March 2002
Reprinted December 2003
Reprinted February 2007
Reprinted January 2008

© David Woodley

The moral right of David Woodley to be identified as the author of this work has been asserted by him in accordance with the Copyright, Designs and Patents Act 1988.

All rights reserved. No part of this publication may be reproduced, stored in a retrieval system, or transmitted in any form or by any means, electronic, mechanical, photocopying, recording or otherwise, without the prior permission of the publisher and copyright owner.

Edited, typeset and published in Gt Britain by:
Léonie Press
an imprint of
Anne Loader Publications
13 Vale Road
Hartford
Northwich
Cheshire CW8 1PL
Tel: 01606 75660 Fax: 01606 77609
e-mail: anne@leoniepress.com
website: www.leoniepress.co.uk

Printed by:
Poplar Services, St Helens
Cover lamination:
The Finishing Touch, St Helens

About the Author

David Woodley worked for 20 years as a prison chaplain, serving in Wormwood Scrubs, Cardiff, Risley and Styal.

Contents

Preface and Acknowledgements i
List of illustrations iii
1. The building of "such a fine place" 1
2. The Chartist prisoners 6
3. The Governor 13
4. The Chaplain 23
5. The Surgeon 32
6. Officers and inmates 38
7. Outside affecting 'Inside' 47
8. Getting tough on criminals 53
9. Power to the centre 60
10. Being local is useful 69
11. Appendix 78
   a. Extracts from Gaol Visiting Register Sept. 1820-Sept. 1915
   b. Rules for The House of Correction dated July 13th 1824
   c. Rules for Misdemeanants in The House of Correction 1840
   d. A Famous Knutsford Hotel

References 92
Index 95

Preface and Acknowledgments

The idea of prison as we understand it is largely a Victorian invention. People were locked up before this but then it was usually to await trial. The travelling assize would empty whatever place people were held. This could be in a local lock-up, a county gaol or even a place used by a local magnate like a bishop. The sentence of the court was usually a physical punishment: often the ultimate one, death. The management of those lock-ups was often sold off for a fee which could be recouped by selling ale to prisoners or relieving, for a money payment, the pains of their irons or fetters.

These muddled arrangements were first brought to public notice when John Howard published his "The State of the Prisons" in 1777. Besides exposing conditions he also made recommendations for how more humanity could be shown. Some of these practical suggestions found their way into Peel's 1823 Prison Act. County authorities were encouraged to improve their local conditions. This encouragement was given more bite when the first Prison Inspectors were appointed in 1837. In their travels around the country they passed on "best practice" and tried to bring consistency of standards. Their work helped to promote the idea of reform as a penal policy - which policy derived much of its strength from evangelical religious conviction. However, when this felt the blast of a general loss of religious faith in the 1850s, those like Lord Carnarvon, who had long been urging a more severe attitude which stressed punishment, came into their own. The 1865 Prison Act incorporated much of the findings of the Carnarvon Committee which advocated the value of harshness as a deterrent. This resulted in a plain diet, monotonous work and generally tough conditions. However, local community leaders were often slow to adopt national policies, sometimes because they had financial implications, sometimes because their experienced suggested other ways and sometimes just to show independence. Those at the centre did not appreciate this resistance and the pressure to centralise increased until it became irresistible in 1878 with the forming of the Prison Commission. In this study I have tried to show how the prison in Knutsford responded to these developments.

To Kathleen Goodchild of Knutsford Historical Society, I acknowledge my debt. She pointed me in the direction of the Cheshire and Chester Archives and Local Studies where the fascinating records of Knutsford Prison are kept. On every occasion I visited, the staff there were always helpful as was Catherine Fell, the librarian at the Prison Service College at Newbold Revel in Warwickshire.

I am also very grateful to Mr J.U. Linley, Governor of Inveraray Jail, Argyll, for allowing me to use three pictures taken from the Jail Guidebook.

My time spent in the Prison Service made it clear to me that then, as now, the problems of managing a prison are very similar – overcrowding; balancing the conflicting aims of punishment and reform; recruiting the right kind of person to look after prisoners; providing education, medical and catering services; respecting the religious needs of those in prison, and over all these, finding the best people to be Governors.

David Woodley
January 2002

List of illustrations

Aerial view taken in 1934 iv

Plan of the Prison.. v

Drawing of the Prison vi

The advertisement for the building of The New House of Correction, The Chester Chronicle, August 1816 3

Detail of a treadwheel in an English prison 9

The crank machine 18

Letter from the bereaved Mrs. Gallop 21

The Governor's new house 31

Dietary advice issued by Home Secretary 35

Exercise yard 37

Warders' houses in Stanley Terrace 39

Prison warders in their uniform 41

Aerial photograph showing proximity of railway.......... 48

Shot drill 55

The Prison in the early 1900s 62

The Sessions House 65

Letter from The Home Office saying the prison buildings were to be transferred to the Army Council 75

Aerial view of the prison taken in 1934, showing how it looked at the end of its life. (Aerofilms Series 19444, courtesy of Knutsford Historical Society).

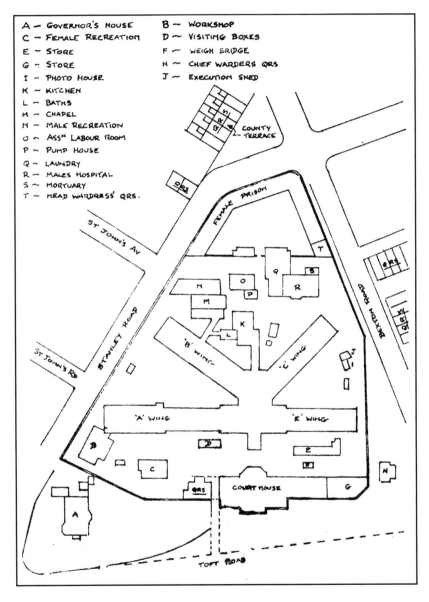

Plan of the Prison. (From an article by Will Strachan in Knutsford Historical and Archaeological Association Journal)

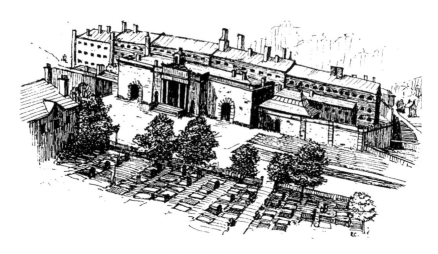

Knutsford Prison.
(Drawing courtesy of Knutsford Historical Society).

Chapter One

THE BUILDING OF 'SUCH A FINE PLACE'

The population of England in 1811 was 11,000,000, in 1851 it was over 21,000,000. With this growth went distress for many. When the army was demobilised after Waterloo, disorder and crime often followed those who found it impossible to obtain work. In the countryside enclosure had been completed and the rural ways turned upside down in the attempt to provide food and labour for the cities and growing industries. The movement from country to town and city upset the fabric of society which had given stability and certainties to be relied on. Uncertainties fueled the riots and disturbances by those known as Luddites who broke up the machinery threatening jobs in the countryside and disturbed the peace of the new industrial areas. The swollen towns were full of young people who, when faced with the difficult economic and social problems of urban living, had few personal resources to meet them. The result of all this was "an upsurge of crime which was the fruit of a society in rapid transition".

With society's institutions under threat, punishment and prisons seemed to many the only way of holding back the chaos of disorder. In Cheshire, however, the prison at Chester was overcrowded and The House of Correction at Middlewich small and in need of repair. James Neild, a keen observer of prisons, had visited Middlewich and his published 'State of the Prisons' of 1812 made the following comments:

"The employment of the prisoners consists of weaving,

shoemaking, picking oakum, batting cotton and spinning jersey: and all of them, who formally had but one third, have now one half of their earnings; the other half is accounted for to the County.

"When a prisoner comes in ragged and dirty, he is stripped, and undergoes ablution in the bath: the County clothing is then put on, his own clothes washed, boiled in alum and water, mended, and laid by for him till he goes out.

"The whole prison is whitewashed at least twice a year, the sleeping and day rooms oftener; and good water is accessible at all time. Every part of the building is consequently very clean. Scales and weights are provided by the County; and I found the loaves supplied to the prison of full weight. All the courtyards here are well paved with flagstones: and being on a inclined plane, soon become dry again after wet weather and are easily kept clean.

"The humane and very attentive Constable of Chester Castle was for many years the Keeper of this Gaol. His faithful conduct, at length, has raised him to the important trust which he now meritoriously discharges, as an excellent example to his successors. Its influence here remains. The present Keeper of this County Bridewell is both intelligent and active and appears in all respects well calculated for his situation.

"Every attention is here paid by considerate Magistrates, which the sorrows and sufferings of wholesome confinement can require".[1]

Neild appears to have visited on two occasions and notes the number of prisoners: November 20th 1801 – 21 prisoners, and October 13th 1805 – 26 prisoners. The pressure of prisoners in Cheshire which led to the need for additional cells is seen in the Annual Account of the Gaols, Houses of Correction and Penitentiaries in England and Wales for 1819; it records the number of prisoners committed to Middlewich as 708.

Faced with this problem the authorities decided on July 16th 1811 that a new Sessions House, Grand Jury Room and a New House of Correction for the reception of 150 prisoners should

TO ARCHITECTS, BUILDERS, &c.

AN Order having been made at the last General Quarter-Sessions of the Peace for the county of Chester, held at Nether Knutsford, in the said county, on the 16th July instant, that a NEW SESSIONS HOUSE, GRAND JURY ROOM, and other conveniences; and also, a NEW HOUSE OF CORRECTION, for the reception of 150 Prisoners, with a DWELLING HOUSE, and suitable accommodations for a Keeper, should be immediately built in a convenient situation near the said town of Nether Knutsford; and a Committee of Magistrates having been appointed, for the purpose of carrying the said order into effect; Architects or Builders, willing to furnish PLANS for such Buildings as before-mentioned, are requested to send the same, with an estimate of the expense of completing such Buildings, sealed up, to the Office of Messrs. LEEKE and POTTS, in the City of Chester, on or before 26th day of August next, in order that the same may remain unopened, until the 29th day of the said month of August, when a meeting of the said Committee, will be held at Nether Knutsford aforesaid, for taking such Plans and Estimates, into consideration. And, as an encouragement to any persons who may furnish such Plans and Estimates, the Committee has directed, the following Rewards to be given, viz:—

To the person who shall furnish the Plan which shall be the most approved of by the Committee, together with an Estimate, the sum of £50.

For the next best Plan, with an Estimate, the sum of £40.

And, for the next best Plan, with an Estimate, the sum of 30L.

Chester, July 20th, 1816.

The advertisement for the building of The New House of Correction, The Chester Chronicle, August 1816

"be immediately built in a convenient situation near the town of Nether Knutsford". Advertisements were placed in local and national newspapers. The plans of Mr. George Moneypenny of London were chosen. His estimate of £30,814 was accepted and he was also awarded the £50 prize for the best plan. Moneypenny had already some experience in the building of prisons having been responsible for Leicester Gaol in 1790-2, Winchester Gaol in 1805, Exeter House of Correction in 1807-9 and alterations to Petworth Prison in 1816.

People often had mixed feelings about a prison being built in their locality. Local traders, while hoping to gain business, also feared that the bad smells associated with prisons would drive away customers. Believing as they did that disease was spread through the pollution of the air, prisons often seemed to pose a health hazard and discharged prisoners having to pass through their town added to their anxiety.

Nevertheless the plans progressed with Mr. William Heap of Manchester gaining the tender for bricklaying, carpentry and masonry in February 1817 and work beginning in the Spring. It was a major project involving large quantities of bricks being made locally and sandstone being brought from Runcorn. By October 1819 things were going wrong. It became obvious that Moneypenny's original estimate was far too low. In order to complete the building an additional £16,000 would be needed. The committee of Magistrates concluded that they had been deceived and he was dismissed. William Heap continued until the end of the year when he too asked for more money and was sacked. So by the end of 1819 there was no Architect, no Supervisor of Works and unpaid bills. Mr Heap did not accept the Magistrates' sacking of him quietly. The records have sixty one pages detailing his claims for expenditure on labour and materials.[2] Much of the dispute revolved around the costs involved in transporting stone from Runcorn by barge to Wincham and then transferring it into carts for the final journey to Knutsford. Much of the detail seems to have involved trying to blacken Heap's character. It was claimed that he "has not had much business for several years and that he is not a man of very fair character". When examination revealed his failure to keep records such as a Journal or Daybook, the comment "a man of credit upon so large an undertaking would have kept one" was made. Adjectives like "fictitious", "fraudulent", and "unprofessional" were freely linked to his actions. Heap's witnesses received similar treatment. Gillman, a boatman involved in the transshipment of stone at Wincham, "has been more than once in custody at the New Bailey Manchester

THE BUILDING OF 'SUCH A FINE PLACE'

on charges of Felony and that after his examination before the referees he told a person that Heap had promised to give him the boat be commanded if he brought him well through Knutsford." Mr. Bateson, whom Heap had used as an architect, "was not an architect but a surveyor and never did any large buildings". Despite these attempts to undermine his supporters, Heap did win his case and was ordered to receive the £19,647.6s.9d owed to him.

All these difficulties did not prevent the building being completed. Indeed *The Countryman's Rambler* makes this comment on it: "Was a building so high in renown, That a Lord might live there, but one hardly believes, That such a fine place, was built only for thieves".

The actual date of opening is not clear but the Gaol Visiting Register starts in September 1820 (see Appendix, page 78).

We can gain some idea of what went on in the prison from the Rules dated July 3rd 1824 and the seven volumes of Minutes of Visiting Justices which begin on November 20th 1826. Present at this first meeting were the Chairman, George Legh, Sir John Stanley, Sir Henry Mainwaring, Egerton Leigh and Sir Thomas Parker. Instructions were issued about the working of the treadwheel and crank mills. The Committee's Clerk Mr. Roscoe was ordered to make a comparison of The House of Correction Rules with recent Acts of Parliament on the regulation of gaols so that he could help the Keeper in drawing up new Rules. The senior Officer, Mr. Hudson, pointed out the need for a room for visits. He was instructed to look into this and also given the responsibility of supervising the opening of all parcels sent in for prisoners. Provision of a stove for the cleaning of prisoners' clothes was set in motion as was a full inventory of everything in the prison belonging to the County. On that day there were 232 prisoners.[3]

Chapter Two

THE CHARTIST PRISONERS

The *Manchester Times* of January 17th 1837 reported that there were 5,000 workers either unemployed or on short time. Despite slight improvement over the next two years there was unemployment in areas of Lancashire and the Midlands, sufficient to provide a seedbed for trouble from all sections of the community. Workers on the land and town traders, landowners and farmers combined in different ways to demand changes. Some joined the Chartists and others the Anti-Corn Law League. Some members were violent in word and action and 665 found themselves in prison charged with "seditious offences or for any offence of a political nature". The treatment they received depended on where they were imprisoned. One of the Chartists, the Revd. Joseph Rayner Stephens, found himself in Chester gaol where he was given a private room to see his family alone each day and had "all the comforts which a man under imprisonment could enjoy". His removal to Knutsford changed all this so much that the judge who had sentenced him intervened when he found the regulations too harsh for a gentleman of education.

All this had a unsettling effect on people and their spirits were raised when 1840 brought improvements, only to fall again the next year. Worse was to follow. "There was no gloomier year in the whole nineteenth century than 1842. Prolonged business difficulties and four years of harvest dearth made England unhappy and afraid, a country of conflict and despair. Bread was dear and flesh and blood were cheap. Movements of protest and revolt swept the country". In the hot summer unemployment, short-term working and a reduction of wages "pressed very severely upon the workpeople".[4] Queen Victoria showed her concern by writing to the Archbishop of Canterbury giving permission for collections to be made to provide relief.

Here in Cheshire and Lancashire people began to take direct action to help themselves. Joining in groups they went begging, producing an atmosphere of intimidation which worried the authorities sufficiently that they put troops on standby to aid the civil power. Imagine the feelings of people when on July 21st about 6,000 Staffordshire colliers armed with sticks and bludgeons marched into Congleton demanding food and provisions from shops and houses. Moving on they arrived in Macclesfield where, after their demands for contributions were met, they sabotaged some small coalpits outside the town by pulling out their boiler plugs. Shadowed by the military and an anxious body of magistrates they arrived in Poynton where the heat seems to have gone out of the protest, much to the authorities' relief.

The next tense moment came in August at the anniversary of Peterloo. Then workers remembered the day in 1819 when eleven of their colleagues were killed and more than 400 wounded at a demonstration in St Peter's Field, Manchester. Peaceful but disgruntled weavers had been dispersed by the regular cavalry on the orders of jittery magistrates resulting in what came to be known as the "massacre of Peterloo" - an allusion to the Battle of Waterloo. Fortunately the anniversary did not spark off further trouble as feared.

Nevertheless these incidents, which came to be known as the Plug Riots, were followed by arrests. As the confidence of the authorities had been shaken the sentences were severe. At a special Commission of Assize held in Chester on October 1842, forty-five people were sentenced to imprisonment, seven on charges of conspiracy. They were taken to Knutsford and the treatment they received became the subject of an investigation by Captain Williams, an Inspector of Prisons.

KNUTSFORD PRISON – THE INSIDE STORY

In March 1843, Thomas Dunscombe, a Chartist M.P., wrote to the Home Secretary complaining about the diet and discipline at the prison. One of the prisoners, William Wright, was singled out "as dangerously ill and that his health is sinking under the discipline and dietary of the prison". The Visiting Justices' response was to request a report from the prison Surgeon, Richard Deane. He claimed that Wright's dyspepsia had been treated *"with some stomach medicine and his oatmeal gruel substituted for by 8oz of bread night and morning".*[5] In addition Magistrates who saw the prisoners concluded, *"from the personal appearance of Wright he does not appear to be out of health or to be suffering from the discipline or diet of the Gaol".*[6] Dissatisfied with this, Sir James Graham, the Home Secretary, dispatched the Prison Inspector to Knutsford.[7] He took care to a adopt a procedure which gave a better chance of getting nearer to the truth, insisting that the Governor, Mr Burgess, be absent when the evidence was given. Only after it had been gathered was it read to him, then he could cross-examine witnesses and call witnesses on his own behalf. Ten prisoners and eight officers from Knutsford, together with the Chaplain and the Surgeon were questioned. In addition two officers from Chester and one of the Visiting Justices, Harry Mainwaring, were interviewed.

The evidence found that the Governor had indeed used strong language when the Chartist prisoners arrived at the gaol. "You are sent here to be punished and you shall be punished" and "the strongest man among you won't have a constitution that I would give twopence for when your sentence shall expire". These words were heard by prisoners and officers but the Inspector concluded "they had been a caution to prevent breaches of the regulations and to impress his authority upon the prisoners". He found the general attitude of the Governor was "to be attentive to the complaints of the prisoners and humane in his general conduct".

The Inspector felt that using the treadmill and prisoners on it as a peepshow was objectionable. In evidence Thomas

Bramall of Stockport, a prisoner, said: "I have frequently been called out to go upon the mill to show ladies and gentlemen who are visitors". The Knutsford Magistrates ordered the practice to stop, stating that "prisoners shall not be exhibited to visitors".

Much time was devoted to the question of the diet. Even the doctors felt that the diet was insufficient for those prisoners serving long sentences but they had not shared their concerns with the Magistrates who visited the gaol. Instead they

Detail of a treadwheel in an English prison. (Reproduced by kind permission of Inveraray Jail, Argyll).

had used their discretion and increased the diets of those needing it. Their failure to see each prisoner twice a week meant that they had not noticed the general bad effects. Defending themselves, the doctors pointed out that over the past year only two prisoners had died which suggested good general health. Their knowledge of the diet at other prisons suggested that in comparison Knutsford's *"is not only as nutritious but more so than in most other prisons"*. Drawing on his fifteen years of experience looking after the health of prisoners Richard Deane reckoned, *"it is impossible to keep men under long sentence of imprisonment in robust health; it is not that they fall actually sick, but they become pallid, careworn and enfeebled and lose their energy and exertion. This is not the effect of the diet, or the labour, the locality or the discipline of the gaol, but arises I believe solely from their* being in confinement and the depressing circumstances attending that confinement".[8] He followed up this modern diagnosis with an equally modern prescription. *"The prisoners sentenced to twelve months confinement and upwards have been allowed an additional half pound of bread daily and two oz. of cheese twice in each week. They appear to relish their cheese very much and so far as I can at present form a judgement of the effect of the increase it is likely to be attended with advantage. I did not recommend the increase in food either in consequence of or in apprehension of sickness in the gaol, but in the hope that the prisoners would be cheered and pleased by the indulgence and having consequently suffered less from the depression attendant on their imprisonment they would be on leaving the gaol, in a better state for entering upon habits of labour and industry."*[9]

Despite this thoughtful approach to his responsibility, he was censured by the Inspector for his slackness in the routine treatment of sick prisoners. One of the hospital nurses admitted: *"I have given Epsom salts a great many times without having the specific directions of the medical officer".*[10] The Governor also came in for criticism about his too frequent restricting of the diet as a form of punishment. His allowing the Taskmaster to decide punishments in his absence, and then inking them in as his decision when he returned, was to stop. In future daily exercise should not be reduced by half to thirty minutes and the prison rules should be exhibited around the prison for all prisoners to see.

This investigation by central government, in the person of Sir James Graham, shows determination to secure "consistency and utmost practical uniformity" in prison regimes. Local government may provide the finances, and local Magistrates the immediate supervision of diet and discipline, but they and the superior officers of Governor, Surgeon and Chaplain were subject to inspection.

The findings of the Inspector did not show Mr. Edward Burgess, the Governor, in a good light. Three years before he had been severely reprimanded for over-ruling the Surgeon when on medical grounds he wanted to have the flogging of

Edward Turner, a 14-year-old prisoner, stopped. Now the local Magistrates re-affirmed their confidence in him despite his lapses. In his favour they referred to the Inspector's recent comments on his efficiency. *"The books and accounts... are most admirably kept, they reflect great credit... I think so highly of them... and recommend them as well worthy of adoption in other prisons"*. The Home Secretary on the other hand felt that the Governor's recent lapses must *"deprive him of their confidence. He believed the decision would lead to evil consequences detrimental to the maintenance of good order in prisons and calculated to lessen the confidence which Parliament has been disposed to impart to Magistrates in the superintendence and regulation of gaols."*[11] The Knutsford Visting Magistrates remained unmoved in their support of their man.

The Chaplain, the Reverend William Robert Browne, who had served them since 1840, did not retain their support. His duties meant that he attended the prison daily for about five hours. It appears that early on in his appointment he disagreed with the Magistrates as to the nature of these duties and he seems not to have had good relations with the Governor. In 1810 the Holford Committee appointed by Parliament recognised that in the closed world of prison there needed to be safeguards against the Governor's misuse of authority. They saw the Chaplain as "the most obvious channel of complaint if the Governor be concerned in the supposed injury". To do this he "must occasionally confer with the prisoner without the presence of the Governor". It is clear that this confidentiality could be the source of annoyance especially if linked with a wide interpretation of the area of responsibility. The Magistrates felt that the Chaplain had overstepped what they felt was his duty and requested him *"to confine himself to his spiritual duties"*. Mr. Brown felt this was a restraint but they insisted that he was *"to make a report on the state of the gaol and any observation he has on the discipline"*.[12]

Obviously the atmosphere within the prison must have been affected by these tensions. The Chaplain was a witness at the enquiry into the treatment of the Chartists and his evidence seems fair and balanced towards the Governor. During his evidence he admitted that in addition to the official journal of duties he kept a private journal. This fact played an important part in the local Visiting Magistrates' attitude to him. As the Chaplain was paid by the Magistrates, they could not see how any information gained by him "in confidence" should be witheld from them.

On receipt of the Inspector's report they expressed themselves in this way: *"In going through this investigation the visiting justices have had the conduct of the Chaplain brought prominently before them and are sorry to report that it has been such as to meet with their general condemnation... there has been constant dissension betwixt the Governor and himself. The visiting justices have from time to time heard complaints and admonished and advised him but without effect. His demeanor has led to a total want of that co-operation which is essential to the discipline of a gaol and whilst he personally attends within the gaol the prescribed number of hours each day the visiting justices are satisfied that a very considerable portion of that time is devoted to other purposes than his duties. He has conducted himself in a very unsatisfactory way before the visiting justices on this investigation almost shutting out any inquiry at their hands. Sheltering himself under some sort of confidential communication to the Inspector of Prisons which the visiting justices cannot understand, as they believe that whatever has been communicated to him relative to the gaol should have been communicated to them. He has admitted to the keeping of a private journal in which there are entries relative to the gaol which he refuses to show and the visiting justices are so satisfied that so long as he remains an officer of the gaol the proper discipline cannot be maintained. They have concluded to represent his conduct and demeanor to the Court of Quarter Sessions and to recommend his discharge".*[13]

Chapter Three

THE GOVERNOR

—	1833	*Mr. Christmas*
1833 – 1844		*Mr. Edward Burgess*
1844 – 1877		*Mr. George Gallop*
1877		*Captain Talbot-Price RN*
	1898	*Captain Pennethorn*
1898 – 1899		*Captain Connor*
1899		*Major Nelson*

Prisons are intriguing because of the people involved: those who are responsible for the running of the institution – governors, doctors, chaplains and prison officers – and those who are sentenced to a time "inside". The hidden nature of imprisonment makes us curious or morbidly interested. So what were the Governors of Knutsford like?

On 8th April 1844 the Visiting Magistrates decided that Edward Burgess should be removed: *'it is inexpedient that he should continue'*. Having stood by him against the Home Secretary over the complaint of the Chartist prisoners, they let him go over complaints that he used prison labour for his own benefit. The record contains eight pages of evidence from prisoners and staff. Apparently he used them to paint his property and remove manure for use in his garden. Some scrap iron belonging to the prison and so County property was reused for his personal use. This petty pilfering was outrageous behaviour and inconsistent with the respectability and gentility demanded from a public servant. The record of 30th March noted that Mr. Burgess's action *"wanted proper attention to gaol regulations"*. Between these dates and June 15th, advertisements would have been placed in local and national newspapers, resulting in 42 applications.

What sort of man would the Magistrates have been looking for? Times had changed since John Clay, chaplain of Preston Gaol, could write "a rough and ready bully, with a flavour of good nature and wit enough to manage the prison cheaply, was the kind commonly approved by justices". That was in 1820. The status of prison governors had improved: the change of the title Keeper or Gaoler to Governor signalled this in 1839. Thomas le Breton, one of the new breed of Governors, could list the desirable characteristics of a Governor as "firmness, cool deliberation, some education and considerable knowledge of human nature". Hoping to find such a man the Magistrates short-listed five. Of these four were ex-military, indicating the Knutsford justices' acceptance of the general conviction that the experience of a military man in dealing with the control of men and stores, would be useful in prison organisation. However this commonly held view did not carry the day and on July 1st 1844 Mr. George Gallop, the only non-military candidate, was appointed Keeper. (Knutsford had yet to implement The Act for the Better Ordering of Prisons). His salary of £350 was in the top group of prisons for pay. Like most other Governors he would have been provided with a house, coals and candles and perhaps a provision of bread, soap, potatoes and other vegetables, washing of clothes, taxes and a garden or field. Recalling perhaps, how manure for his field had played a part in Mr. Burgess's fall from grace, Mr. Gallop was required *"to provide bonds to the sum of £500 from two persons for his good behaviour"*.[14]

For 32 years the prison at Knutsford was governed by George Gallop. The Minutes of the Visiting Magistrates enable us to get some idea of the problems he had to face. The underlying question in any prison at this time was "Silent or Separate?" A prison run on the Silent system forbade any communication between prisoners. All activities, work, exercise, even going to chapel were done in silence under the gaze of vigilant officers who would prevent even sign language. Separate conditions meant each prisoner had a cell in which he lived and did his work. Exercise involved wearing a hood so you couldn't be identified and in the chapel you sat in an individual box. Both systems had come out of the experience of American prisons and each had its English supporters. After some consideration the Magistrates decided in 1835 to adopt the version of the Silent system in use in Wakefield prison with the proviso, *"as far as the present means within the prison will permit"*.[15] The expense of implementing the theory that separation would reform came about in the cost of building cells and employing supervisory officers. Local Magistrates, conscious of the need to keep local rates low, were always aware of costs. A previous Governor, Mr. Christmas, had been worried that weaving as a job for prisoners provided too many opportunities for conversation and a breaking of the silence. He advised that it should be stopped. The Magistrates, aware that the prisoners' weaving produced income for the prison, considered this in 1838 and refused. They offered a compromise that the looms be put in the cells where isolated prisoners could weave in the required silence.

The individual prisoner's introduction to Knutsford Gaol would have been to hear the Governor reading the regulations. "Silence: no singing, whistling, attempting to communicate by signs or in any other way. Either in the day rooms, or cells any unnecessary looking about in going to or returning from chapel or at meals work or exercise." Providing the necessary isolation inevitably required alterations and additions to prison buildings. Throughout his time as Governor, Mr. Gallop had to deal with the Prison Inspectors who urged more separate cells and the local Magistrates who were uneasy about how much it could cost. They might conclude in 1839 that *"boys could with advantage be separate from adults"*. But it wasn't until 1846 when the Magistrates of each county prison were required to investigate in detail the costs, that the Governor and architect were instructed to report on how much it would cost to adapt Wards 1 & 2. Their plans, costed at £3,000 and approved by Major Jebb, the London-based Supervisor of Prison Building, were finally approved in 1847. The next year when the Prison Inspector visited he was pleased to report: *"The alterations in one of the main wings of the prison, with a view to converting it into separate cells, have been completed and 70 new cells have thus been constructed, which vary in length from 10 to 10½ feet, in breadth from 5½ to 9 feet and in height 10-11 feet."*

The desirability of separating females came in for the same questioning as to costs. Two plans were put forward in 1850. One was to erect a building within the present boundary at the cost of £1,355 and a more ambitious one was to build outside the present boundary but linked with existing buildings. This would provide 50 separate female places and free up 44 existing cells for use by male prisoners. The cost of this, being £9,265, ruled it out despite its obvious advantages. However prison plans often have to be adapted to circumstances, in this case the authorities in Chester wishing Knutsford to take on responsibility to house debtors. They were prepared to give a grant of £10,000 to build outside the present prison boundary. The Knutsford Magistrates saw the plan as a way of increasing male cell accommodation. It was discussed on April 5th and by September 20th they were considering plans for a new female wing costing £11,760 and advertising for tenders in local and London papers. This change may have been the result of Jebb's interventions mentioned on April 19th. The Magistrates noted that although Jebb couldn't visit Knutsford he would look at the plans if they were sent to him and give advice. The result of all this was that in June 1855 they could report: *"The new part of the prison is now in a fit state for the reception of female prisoners. The justices are ready to proceed with alterations of the present female wing for reception of County Court debtors."*[16]

Disagreement over whether the Separate system was the better penal policy was real. The government might be in favour but their Prison Inspectors were not equal in their enthusiasm as to how it should be implemented. Captain Williams, who inspected Knutsford on several occasions, was not totally convinced. Maybe it was he who gave rise to the rather pained comment of the justices that after all their efforts and all the expense of building *"the altered views of persons in authority with reference to accommodation... has rendered it so far ill adapted"* – they had failed to provide in-cell water and W.C.

Of course separating prisoners did make a difference to the kind of work you could get them to do. Some saw work as a means of usefully occupying prisoners during their long hours of imprisonment. Teaching a new skill like weaving or basket-making might be a way of helping them to earn an honest living after release. If you were keen on reforming the wayward this would be attractive. If you were a magistrate with an eye on costs the income from this kind of prisoners' work would influence your attitude. In 1855 when the Governor reported there were two basket-makers among the prisoners this was seen as a potential source of income made from sales. A prison officer was to be trained to teach the skill so as to have basket making as a prison job. The Magistrates' enthusiasm of April was stifled by October when they discovered there were rules against retailing goods produced by prisoners. Perhaps they looked back to earlier days when for example Preston prison was known to be full of 'busy scenes of cheerful industry' and the profits from weaving had enabled the county rates for each prisoner to be reduced to 3d per day.

Against this 'commonsense' view that work was a useful way of filling the time of prisoners, there were those who believed prison work should be punitive and add to the unpleasantness of imprisonment. Sidney Smith, the social commentator, expressed the feelings of many when he said there had to be a monotony and uselessness in prison work to make it a punishment. Holford, an M.P., gave his opinion that "work which is to produce profit will run counter to discipline and moral improvement". In separate cells there was a crank which "ground nothing but air". Individuals were set a target for the number of turns per day. Often, as in 1839 they were reported as "out of service because not in good repair". An alternative in Knutsford was woolpicking, regarded "as irksome an employment as any used". A more communal hard labour could be exacted on the treadmill. This device was invented by William Cubbit following an old principle used in monasteries to pump water. Prisoners spent hours stepping up the series of stairs which dropped under them.

The crank machine. (Reproduced by kind permission of Inveraray Jail).

The rigour of this depended on the height individual prisons laid down. In York they demanded 6,000 ft every day, "equal to climbing Mount Ararat". Stafford prisoners had to climb the equivalent of "half the height of Everest or 16,630 ft". Knutsford's rate is unknown but unlike many treadmills that were used to "grind the wind" and so emphasise the uselessness of the work, the Magistrates used it to pump water for the prison. As can be imagined its constant use made for much wear and tear and in October 1848 the Magistrates were informed that *"the treadmill was in great need of repair"* and that water now had to be pumped by crank labour. They were aware that the treadmill had its critics who claimed that it damaged prisoners whose diet was inadequate for such demanding work. One medical opinion said "men forced to this labour fall off greatly... both in health and strength before quitting the prison, they shrink very much in size and look pale". With this in mind they resolved that the treadmill should not be repaired. Within six months and after the Governor had reported on the relative merit of crank labour and hard wheel labour they authorised a Mr.Woods to carry out repairs to crank and treadmill costing £602 10s 11d. Their preference was for the treadmill as it occupied more prisoners. Those *"who from physical defects or other causes might be considered unfit persons to be employed on the treadmill could find occupation at the crank"*. Here we can see the pressure of how to occupy prisoners bearing down on the Governor and Magistrates.

In the earlier days (1828) of using the treadmill in Knutsford it is interesting to note that it was decided to use the system adopted in Gloucester prison. The more humane practice of allowing individuals, after their time on the treadmill, to sit down and rest was discontinued in favour of forcing them to walk around in a circle. There was to be no rest for the wicked! On 22nd February 1839 the Visiting Justices record that *"the present mode of employment is the best that can be adopted"*.[17] Trying to balance on one hand the feeling that work should be useful and productive, and on the other the demand for punitive labour that would deter, the comment is a sigh from the harassed administrator. Being local the Magistrates were sensitive to local public opinion: the voice of the ratepayers who helped finance the prison. They would have been interested to know that in 1832 the average cost of maintaining each prisoner was reduced from 2s 7d a week to 2s 4d. Some would have felt strongly that the productive labour by prisoners could reduce this cost. Others would have preferred to know that the prison work was disliked. Work was a constant problem. In 1875 when the Magistrates discovered that the annual earnings of the prisoners per head for the past year had been £2 19s 0d – an improvement of 3s – the Deputy Governor responsible was praised and had his salary increased from £120 to £150.

The main responsibility of any Governor was to maintain order within the prison. Discipline was enforced and sometimes there was a need to resort to physical punishment. Under

Mr. Burgess on 22nd February 1839, it was reported: *"Joseph Dalton – 12 yrs old a convicted felon was ordered to receive 12 lashes on the breech for refusing work on woolpicking: He has frequently been reported for misconduct."* In 1845 on January 11th: *"A boy John Gatley to be flogged in the presence of other boys of the prison"*.[18]

We get some idea of the nature of these punishments in the Inspector's 1837 report. "Whip handle 18 inches long, nine lashes 21 inches long, with nine single knots each. The whipping is inflicted by the beadle of the parish, who receives two shillings for each punishment. I witnessed the infliction of this punishment upon five boys, sentenced to be whipped at the previous sessions. Four received 3½ dozen and the fifth four dozen, which is the ordinary number inflicted unless the Surgeon interferes, who is always present. The punishment was as severe as that which I have witnessed in the army, but I do not consider it to have been excessive. They are generally sent to the hospital afterwards for a day or two, more as a measure of precaution than of necessity".[19]

In the matter of punishments the Magistrates were not slow to voice their opinion. In 1851 they discovered *"that a Gag and Bridle has on one or two occasions within the last 7 years been used on female prisoners"*.[20] Their opinion was that it was a practice open to question legally and they ordered it to be discontinued. They pointed out to Mr. Gallop in 1854 that he should not deprive a prisoner of exercise for more that a week without their authority

To succeed in maintaining a peaceful and well-run prison demanded much of any man. Mr. Christmas was Governor until 1835 when he was dismissed for administrative slackness. The main cause of this charge seems to have been his use of materials belonging to the County and using prisoners' labour to manage a piece of land. He had excused them work on the treadmill and used them instead to make his hay and repair his hedges. We have seen how Mr. Burgess fell foul of similar charges. Mr. Gallop served Knutsford well for many years but

THE GOVERNOR

Knutsford
April 2nd 1877.

To the Chairman & Visiting
Justices of the House of Correction
Knutsford

Gentlemen

Allow me to thank you for the very kind manner in which you expressed to me your great sympathy in the address you sent me from the Meeting on the great loss I had sustained in the death of my late Husband Mr George Gallop.

I take this opportunity to thank you very much for the great kindness and consideration you have shown to me since my Husband's death which I shall for ever remember.

I remain
Gentlemen,
Yours Obediently
Charlotte Gallop

Letter from the bereaved Mrs. Gallop (Chester Record Office) even he found himself accused along similar lines. In 1851 the charge that he had used prisoner labour to clip his pony was investigated. It was found that he had in fact paid 12s 6d to the County for the work done. All this happened weeks after the upheaval caused by the resignation of the Deputy Governor after 24 years' service, the Schoolmaster resigning and several officers being dismissed. This had started on the complaint of a discharged prisoner Joseph Powell. An enquiry found that officers had been using leather belonging to the County and getting prisoners to make shoes which were then sold outside the prison. Supervision had been lax on the part of the Deputy Governor who was described *"as advanced in years and almost past duty"*. They must have been sensitive to the Governor needing support during this time of difficulty and merely urged him *"to take more vigilance"*, realising *"as might have been expected the removal of so many officers has been attended with considerable excitement amongst the prisoners inasmuch as they consider it a triumph gained over the authorities of the prison"*.[21] Despite acts of malicious damage to prison property there was confidence that things would calm down and "the prison and its inmates fall into their usual and orderly course". That it did rested with Mr. Gallop. In January of 1877 he tendered his resignation on grounds of ill health and died on February 5th. The group who had appointed him 32 years before – the Visiting Magistrates – wanted to *"express their sympathy and condolence with the widow and family and to record the great respect in which Mr. Gallop was held during the long period of his office"*.[22]

Chapter Four

THE CHAPLAIN

1834 – 1840 *The Revd. Peter Vannett*
1840 – 1843 *The Revd. William Robert Browne*
1843 – 1868 *The Revd. Charles Mitchell*
1868 – 1907 *The Revd. William Truss*
1907   *The Revd. John Roulby*

People in prison have always received the consolations of religion when in need. In 1777 when John Howard visited the prisons in England he was pleased to note that most justices of the peace were complying with the 1773 Act of Parliament allowing them to appoint and pay Chaplains to their prisons. Often prison work had to be fitted around the duties of a parish priest or teacher in a local school. The return for Knutsford in 1832 lists the Chaplain's duties as *"Prayers and a sermon twice on Sundays. Prayers are read daily in each day room and in the chapel on Wednesdays and Fridays prayers and a lecture. Prisoners are taught to read and provided with Bibles by the Chaplain'.*[23]

In this period most ministers of the Established Church would be classed as 'gentlemen' a fact that gave rise to doubts in the mind of The Inspector General of Prisons in France. When he visited England in the late 1830s he commented: "The Anglican minister is a gentleman, which is why he has but little influence on the lowest ranks of the social classes. The prisoner feels untouched by the broad statements of dogma he hears proclaimed from the pulpit on high." However lasting his influence, prisoners could not avoid him. Attendance at a religious service was compulsory and there was no escape from his visiting

The early decades of the nineteenth century placed the Chaplain in a very influential position. Society as a whole was greatly influenced by the Evangelicals and their beliefs in the power of religion to change the lives of individuals found support from those responsible for prisons. Prison rules and regimes were geared to the observance of regular religious exercises by which they were convinced prisoners could be reformed. Reform as a principle guided much penal policy but was resisted by those who believed more in the punitive aspects of imprisonment to deter individuals from anti-social behaviour. Chaplains often found themselves in the middle of this battlefield of conflicting ideas. However their views were listened to by the men who made the decisions. In Knutsford the Magistrates puzzled over the rival systems of Silence or Separation, both developed in America and influencing English ideas. They received a report from the Chaplain Peter Vannett on April 4th 1834 who in his contact with prisoners noted: *"Many are daily heard expressing regret and openly avowing their determination through God's help to turn from their evil courses."*[24] He questions the value of deterrence, *"conduct from compulsion cannot be depended on. Even the severe system of solitary confinement in America is found to fail."* He said that individuals kept returning to prison despite the hardship of the experience and instanced a 13-year-old boy already on his third sentence of imprisonment. His long experience suggested imprisonment did harm. This modern view made him *"of the opinion that it ought to be avoided as much as possible and were the legislation to invest Magistrates with a discretionary power to imprison or order restitution with or without a fine for offences particularly if committed by youths."* He believed the effect would be obvious in the depopulation of prisons. Such views would find a place in the minds of Magistrates conscious of the costs of running a prison. Indeed at the same meeting they were congratulating themselves at having *"succeeded with due attention to the health and proper dieting of prisoners in reducing the cost of maintenance from 1s 7d to 1s 5d per head per week."*

Nevertheless the following year they decided to adopt the Silent system as practised at Wakefield. They had a prison to run and in any case any penal philosophy carried a proviso *"as far as the present means within the gaol will permit"*. Compromise of principle has its effect and perhaps this was at the back of the Chaplain's comment of June 27th about the general atmosphere among prisoners: *"perhaps the increasing strictness of discipline and the lowness of diet may have had some effect".*[25] The decision to run Knutsford according to the Silent system required an efficient Governor so it is interesting to note that it was about this time that Mr. Christmas was dismissed for administrative slackness. There appear to have been instances of misuse of official stores: soap, sugar, milk, etc, and excusing prisoners from work on the treadmill to work on the Governor's fences and hay-gathering. His replacement, Mr. Burgess, appears to have been a better organiser but even he needed to be told clearly *"no officer of the prison shall employ in future any of the prisoners as their servants."*[26]

The advocates of the Separate System continued to press their views and many of these were chaplains. John Clay, Chaplain of Preston was a keen spokesman for separation. He believed it reduced the evil influences of association between prisoners. Isolation encouraged reflection and increased opportunity to study. The appointment of the Revd. Whitworth Russell, Chaplain of Millbank Penitentiary, as one of the first Prison Inspectors gave him an opportunity to advocate separation on his visits. All the building projects at Knutsford were influenced by these pressures and despite the costs involved in providing separate cells the numbers were increased. So as in other prisons the 1840s in Knutsford saw an advance of the notion that silence and separation could of themselves create the conditions in which the wicked individuals would repent and reform. The importance of the Chaplain in this is shown in the fact that his salary is the second largest:

in 1832 the Governor's was £280: the Chaplain's £120 and the Surgeon's £100.

The Chaplain visited prisoners – the regulations required him to spend time especially with the sick and those in the punishment cells. Cell to cell visiting was an increasingly difficult task as the prison population was rising. Nevertheless much was expected in this regard. The Prison Inspector's report of 1837 criticised Mr. Vannett and then the Magistrates required him to devote three hours a day in his visits to the Gaol independent of the hours of Divine Service and to visit daily prisoners in solitary cells. It was in this close personal contact that good influence was expected to occur and the knowledge gained gave authority to the Chaplain's opinion that an individual should be give remission of sentence for good conduct. His advice was not always taken as when in 1834 he recommended early release for Slack, a young girl. The Magistrates did not feel that her behaviour deserved their recommendation.

Progressive penal opinion accepted uncritically the link between a lack of education and the commission of crime. Much was made of the fact that new prisoners knew little about religion: "They knew not the name of The Saviour". It was also said: "More of them had heard of Dick Turpin and Jack Shepherd than knew the Duke of Wellington". The programme to improve things came under the Chaplain. At the end of 1833 a schoolmaster and clerk to the Chaplain was appointed. He was to attend for three days of the week and do his work *"so as not to intrude upon punishment according to sentence."* His salary started at £25 a year and progress would bring an additional £35. With the conflict between education as part of the reforming process and the need to be punitive made clear from the start, any success would be difficult. Although the following year the Chaplain supported a request from the schoolmaster for an increase in his hours in the prison, the Magistrates did not support it, even though they were aware that solitary confinement and the demands of the treadmill reduced the opportunities for instruction. A library of books avoided some of these difficulties and so Mr. Vannett proposed obtaining books to the value of £10 from the Christian Knowledge Society. Provided a list of the books purchased was given to them, the Magistrates agreed. Although the Knutsford list is not known it was probably like that given to a Select Committee of the House of Lords in 1835 – titles like 'Directions, Counsels and Cautions', 'Persuasions, in early Piety', 'The Workhouse Boy', and 'Waste not want not' give a flavour of the contents.

Juveniles among the prison population were always targeted for education and in conditions which often failed to keep adults and children separate, there was concern for their moral welfare. In this the Chaplain was much involved, so much so that the Prison Inspector commented in his 1839 report: "It is noticed that here as in other establishments the number of boys sent for slight offences from poor homes appears to be on the increase. I lament the necessity of sending them to prison: e.g. W.S. aged 14 stealing 10 carrots in Congleton workhouse – 1 month's imprisonment. J.H. aged 14 stealing peas to the value of 2d (the property of the overseers of the poor) 2 months imprisonment. The numerous class of boys in this prison not only require the exclusive attention of one officer but a large portion of that of the Chaplain."

In the harsh world where such punishments were accepted, at least the Knutsford authorities allowed the Chaplain to buy spectacles for the use of aged prisoners.

As far as he was able the Chaplain would assist prisoners on their discharge from Knutsford: the reality of this was probably much moral exhortation and a little practical help. Resources for this depended on local charity. In 1844 the welfare on discharge appears to have consisted in one recorded case of clogs, supper and bed at Macclesfield and money for travel to Nottingham. However there were others concerned to give support as was noted at the meeting of the Sessions in October 1849. "The attention of the Chaplain to the moral improvement of the juvenile prisoners has met with the approbation of the Managers of the Philanthropic Farm School through whom some of the boys have been sent to Algoa Bay".

Two years before the Prison Inspector had reported the Revd. Mitchell as believing decent boarding houses for juveniles would prevent many coming into prison in the first place. He noted that over a three-year period "385 persons under 17 years of age have been committed to this prison, 252 from Macclesfield, 102 from Stockport and 30 from Congleton. Out of this number no fewer than 145 were either orphans, illegitimate or deserted by their natural parents. There is no class of society which possesses stronger claims upon our sympathy than the class to which these individuals belong". He pointed out the obvious dangers which awaited these young people and how easy it was to become a victim. "Far be it from me to attempt to justify such wickedness, but it ought to be remembered that human nature is frail and temptation is often strong, even for those who are surrounded by circumstances most favourable to virtue." He proposed well-regulated boarding houses in connection with each factory. "A suitable house might easily be provided and a respectable couple found to preside over it, qualified by possession of humane dispositions to supply the place of parents to deserted children. The inmates would be of course required to pay a reasonable sum for their maintenance." It would be the duty of the master and the matron to mould them into habits of order, economy, cleanliness and honesty. The Chaplain concluded by claiming that all ministers of religion would support these ventures, "by which many would be saved from the temptations to which they are now helplessly exposed and would grow up and continue useful members of society and good Christians".[27]

Whether or not these ideas bore any fruit was not recorded but the problem of individuals being discharged into circumstances which led to further convictions was. Ten years before the Chaplain would have seen many familiar faces arriving in the prison — 144 once before, 83 twice, 14 three times before and 11 four times

Being Chaplain was no easy task especially as the Holford Committee of Parliament in 1810 had concluded: "the most obvious channel of complaint if the Governor be concerned in the supposed injury is the Chaplain". His close personal contacts with prisoners and staff would make him aware of many things and the holder of confidences not to be shared with others holding responsibility in the gaol.

A scandal broke in the prison in September 1834 when one of the women officers, Charlotte Price, accused Mr. Burgess, the Governor, of frequently attempting to seduce her. The Magistrates appear to have jumped to conclusions deciding there and then *"that he has forfeited the confidence of the magistracy and is no longer deserving his situation"*. The Chaplain was criticised for his *"negligence in suppressing circumstances inconsistent with the morality and discipline of the Gaol which has come to his knowledge"*. The matter was left over to their meeting in October by which time things appeared to be different. Charlotte Price's credibility had disappeared and she was *'so utterly worthless that the committee could place no credence in her statements'*. If investigations had cleared the Governor they had exposed the Matron in charge of female prisoners. She apparently had been receiving "frequently a male visitor" and the porter had failed to report this and was dismissed. Charges of withholding information were dropped against the Chaplain although in future he was required to report *"all circumstances coming to his knowledge affecting either the discipline of the gaol or the conduct of any of the officers"*.[28]

We have already seen how this requirement caused the Revd. Browne problems when confronted with the investigations into the treatment of the Chartists in 1843. Any claim to confidentiality was refused him by the Magistrates who instead saw it as an obstruction and worthy of dismissal. However they were prepared to support the Chaplain when in 1849 he complained that a *"Mr Wright of Manchester visited the prison and assembled the female prisoners for the purpose of giving them moral and religious instruction"*. In the same year they recorded *"a very high opinion of the efficiency of Mr Mitchell and the way the various onerous duties of his office are performed... they think that his salary should be increased to £250".*[29] Knutsford Magistrates would have agreed with the commentator who wrote "the Chaplain is part of the system: he lives by it and he is not allowed to interfere with it".

These Magistrates had to provide the prison with a chapel. Attendance was compulsory and the records show that on 26th April 1839 a William Mellor was sentenced to eight days in the solitary cell on a bread and water diet for *"stealing several loaves and wilfully absenting himself from Divine Service"*. Even in the chapel every effort was required to restrict contact between prisoners. In 1832 the Governor reported a need to make changes in the chapel *"to prevent male and female prisoners seeing each other and afford accommodation for all prisoners at once".*[30] The £15 cost of this was agreed. In his 1836 inspection Capt. Williams described the chapel as "of semi-circular form, disposed into parts for females, for felons before trial, for convicted and the gallery for misdemeanants. It is rather small for the number of prisoners and is described as being very close in summer". Three years later the Chaplain was complaining of the need for more space in the chapel and the Magistrates took the advice of Mr Fowles the architect to extend the chapel into one of the rooms of the Governor's house at the cost of £450. The pressure on space was further highlighted: alteration of a female ward would be an opportunity to give the Chaplain a room for interviews in what was now a bathroom – cleanliness giving way to godliness. However the continuing increase in the number of prisoners required more drastic measures. The building of a new chapel was ruled out as too expensive at £1,500. An alternative plan to build the Governor a new house outside the prison walls and incorporate the house which was next to the chapel was accepted. Enlarged, the chapel would have space for 450 sufficient if the population stayed at its current number of more than 300. With this decided in December

THE CHAPLAIN

The Governor's new house

1844 some of the Chaplain's efforts were directed to persuading the authorities to provide a Communion table, cloths, a plated chalice and necessary books. They agreed also that "*he should provide a suitable clock*". All these efforts concluded with an application to the Bishop of Chester for a licence to use the chapel in January 1846. No doubt all concerned were pleased to receive favourable comments when the Inspector visited Knutsford. Nevertheless practical pressures still impacted on divine worship, as the records show: "*The visiting justices think that the time allowed to prisoners for the purposes of attending water closets, exercise and relaxation in the forenoon is scarcely sufficient and they therefore order that the daily service in the chapel shall commence at 9. 30am instead of 9.00am*".[31]

Chapter Five

THE SURGEON

1848 – 1851   Dr. Richard.T. Deane
1851 – 1870   Dr. Charles Merriman
1870 – 1885   Dr. William Sutcliffe
1885   Dr. Theodore Fennell

Such was the fear of disease from association with prison that John Howard, when he was visiting prisons around the country, was banished to the outside seats of the coaches he travelled on. For personal protection he disinfected his notebooks with vinegar. Three years before his 'State of The Prisons' was published in 1777 the Gaol Distemper Act allowed Magistrates to "appoint an experienced Surgeon or Apothecary to attend the prison".

Dr. Deane was the Surgeon in the early years of the gaol at Knutsford. Ventilation and cleanliness were important to him. He saw prisoners on arrival and frequently infection would be observed on the newcomers. The cleaning of individuals by bathing and their clothing by disinfectant was vital. A system was used involving immersion of clothes in strong alum water. This was expensive and not always effective so in October 1832 a request was made for *"disinfecting apparatus on the principle adopted by Dr.Henry"*.[32] It claimed to be effective against cholera and was already in use in the New Bailey in Manchester. The Magistrates ordered that the matter be investigated and particularly to see if existing buildings could house it. £30 was the estimated cost. These enquiries came to nothing and by November 24th the matter was dropped. In 1850 Dr. Deane raised the matter again with the Governor's support. The cost had now risen to £100 but both Manchester and London prisons now used it. *"It consists in throwing by mechanical means a stream of common air, heated at will, to any height that may be desired under 500 degrees, into a disinfecting chamber and thence passing off with any infectious effluvia, by a pipe into the atmosphere"*.[33]

Making sure prisoners and their clothing were clean on arrival was one problem to be coped with. Maintaining cleanliness was another as can be seen in the Magistrates' order of March 1844 *"that blankets used by prisoners be washed at least twice each year and as much oftener as may appear necessary for maintaining a proper degree of cleanliness"*.[34] Most of this washing would have been done by the female prisoners who would have been paid an allowance. In 1831 the Chaplain recommended one shilling a week. The fact that throughout the records there is a regular mention that *"due attention is paid the cleanliness and ventilation of the prison in its various departments"* indicates how important it was.

In individual cases, when required, the Surgeon had to certify individuals as fit to undergo the sentence of transportation or other prison punishment. Here his word could make a great difference. In 1852 he examined two women, Mary Jarvis and Mary Brown, both sentenced to seven years transportation – one for stealing a bed quilt, blanket, shawl and two flatirons and the other for stealing four sovereigns and a shawl. In both cases he recommended clemency. Two years earlier Mary Boon, whom he had passed fit for transportation, was rejected by the medical officer at Millbank in London as suffering from venereal disease. Dr. Deane at Knutsford had judged that she was deliberately feigning to avoid the sentence. Sometimes his authority was questioned nearer home as when he ordered the flogging of 14-year-old Edward Tanner to be stopped and the Turnkey insisted it continue. Such a serious matter required a Magistrates' enquiry. In normal circumstances the Surgeon's opinion was accepted, as in 1856 when *"the punishment of whip-*

ping was not inflicted on John Phillips in consequence of the Surgeon's certjficate that he had a diseased skin".[35] Even the Governor's authority had sometimes to give place to the Surgeon's as Mr. Gallop discovered in 1852 when the Magistrates pointed out: *"It having been stated that the Governor had sent a person to the hospital who was in health, of which the Surgeon had complained. It was ordered that although the Governor had the general superintendence of the hospital as part of the prison yet he should not place any prisoner in health in the hospital without the previous approbation of the Surgeon"*.[36]

It is obvious that diet and health are linked. In prisons this caused a conflict between those who like the Surgeon saw food as part of the process of keeping a good standard of health among prisoners and those who were keen not to make the diet of prisoners better than any group outside who hadn't been convicted of lawbreaking. There was feeling in the public's mind that "the convict had the best diet, the pauper the second best and the soldier the worst". In the early days the food given varied depending on the prison. The Knutsford Magistrates rejected a suggestion made in 1828 to take meat from the diet, confirming their order from a local supplier at 5¼d per pound; although they did a few years later remove the extra allowance. This seemed to be using food as a way of reducing the punitive aspect considered by some to be the point of prison. The dilemma facing those running the prison is seen in May 1835 when the Surgeon reported an increase in sickness, *"Seldom are there less than 20-30 in the hospital as it seems the diet is the cause, it is not sufficiently nutritious and too uniform in its kind. Some variety would be useful"*.[37] The moral value of the Silent system, introduced as a way of emphasising the element of punishment there should be in prison life, had the effect *"of depressing the spirit of prisoners and threatening their general wellbeing"*. The Surgeon's recommendation was that *"a more nutritious diet was advisable"*.[38] With some misgivings, no doubt, the Magistrates ordered that all prisoners should receive one pint of broth made from oxhead on Sundays and Wednesdays. The

DIETARIES of COUNTY and BOROUGH GAOLS 1843.									
	Without Hard Labour.				With Hard Labour.				
Week	Class 1. Less than 7 days.	Class 2. More than 7 days, and not more than 21 days.	Class 3. More than 21 days, and not more than 4 months.	Class 4. More than 4 months.	Class 2. More than 7 days, and not more than 21 days.	Class 3. More than 21 days, and not more than 6 weeks.	Class 4. More than 6 weeks, and not more than 4 months.	Class 5. More than 4 months.
	ozs.	*ozs.*	*ozs.*	*ozs.*	*ozs.*	*ozs.*	*ozs.*	*ozs.*
Bread	112	168	140	168	168	140	168	154
Potatoes	–	–	64	32	–	64	32	112
Meat	–	–	6	12	–	6	12	16
Total Solid Food	112	168	210	212	168	210	212	282
	pints.	*pints.*	*pints*	*pints.*	*pints.*	*pints.*	*pints.*	*pints.*
Soup	–	–	2	3	1	2	3	3
Gruel	14	14	14	14	14	14	14	11
Cocoa	–	–	–	–	–	–	–	3
Total Liquid Food	14	14	16	17	15	16	17	17

Dietary advice issued by the Home Secretary but not compulsory

Surgeon's view on the diet has already been seen in the evidence to the enquiry into the treatment of the Chartist prisoners. It is difficult to know where Knutsford stood in comparison with other prisons but certainly the Surgeon considered it *"not only as nutritious but more so than diets in most other prisons"*.[39] Even so he had to use his discretion in individual cases where necessary and would have preferred a general increase to relieve him of the responsibility. Eventually in 1843 the Home Secretary, Sir James Graham issued a Dietary. Its scale was designed to conform to the principles that "food should be sufficient to maintain health and strength, at the least possible cost... diet ought not to be an instrument of punishment". It had no enforceable authority so some prisons were more generous and some meagre. We do know that it 1844 the Inspector's report on Knutsford said that the prison diet per head per annum cost £5 10s 5½d.

The rules required that Dr. Deane saw each prisoner twice a week and the rising prison population could make this difficult. There was also the fact that prisoners sometimes tried to use the doctor to gain relief from work or a monotonous diet. In the absence of any really effective treatment for many nineteenth century ailments it was normal to prescribe rest or nutritious diet. Prison doctors also used these remedies and here lay the possibility of malingering. Rest from hard labour on the crank or the wheel or the possibility of extra food appealed equally to the sick and the fit, the exhausted and the lazy, to the hungry and the greedy. So in May 1843 he requested an issue of tobacco for someone suffering from a gum complaint. He might have succeeded for this individual but his advice to prevent scurvy generally, by adding onions, soup, sugar and cocoa to the diet, was not taken up by the Magistrates.

Illness easily spread in the close confinement of prison so action had to be taken quickly in June 1847 when there was an outbreak of fever. Additional hospital supervision was recruited and rooms normally occupied by officers were brought into use for the sick. Officers on normal duties around the prison

THE SURGEON

Exercise yard. (Reproduced courtesy of Mr Fred MacDowell).

were instructed to avoid unnecessary contact with the sick to avoid spreading the infection. By the end of the month the Justices were able to report to the Quarter Sessions meeting *"the disease has been kept under and there appears little danger of an increase. There has been no deaths and no new cases... the patients now sick of fever are in a state of convalescence"*.[40]

Chapter Six

OFFICERS AND INMATES

Turnkeys, warders and prison officers have been the names given to the group of people in direct daily contact with prisoners. What sort of people decided to do this work? In 1836 the Visiting Inspector listed three Turnkeys all in their fifties, two had formerly been in service while the other was ex-army. Two were mentioned as being able to read and write. They each received a salary of £60 plus coals, candles and soap. Two lived in the prison. Additional male officers were the Taskmaster, the Porter and the Watchman. The Taskmaster was in charge of work, he had served in the 16th Lancers and was paid £90 plus coals, candles, soap and a garden. The Porter, who had 16 years' experience in a London prison, could read and write, and received £60 plus the additions. The youngest man, aged 26 and an ex- miller, served as Watchman for £54 12s 0d. This group of six were responsible for an average 168 prisoners. The 28 females were the responsibility of the Matron, who lived in the prison receiving a salary of £80, assisted by a female Turnkey. The Schoolmaster who served the whole prison was also ex-army and received £60.

The Inspector noted a lack of unity among the prison staff which, as he put it, "excited the attention and investigation of the Magistrates". Officers living within the prison walls were allowed the services of prisoners to clean their houses and tend their gardens. This was not good for discipline, neither was the Turnkeys' "habit of receiving gratuities from the numerous visitors to the prison, which ought, considering the liberal salaries

Warders' houses in Stanley Terrace. An architect's report in 1849 on these to the Magistrates dismissed the complaint of warders' wives that they were smoky. In 1854 it was decided that all warders living outside the prison should no longer receive "an allowance of soap, coal and candles". As a replacement their salaries were increased by £5 a year. This meant that those with one or two years' service received 21s per week rising to 25s after eight years.
(From the collection of Knutsford Historical Association)

paid them, be strictly forbidden".[41] The decision of the Magistrates in April 1843 to discontinue the practice of keeping a cow within the prison for the purposes of providing milk for the officers indicated a tightening tip of the disciplinary nature of prisons. This continued in October 1844 when it was decided that the officers were to have a uniform of "cap, coat and trowsers". Officers would be responsible for providing the cloth and the uniforms would be made up in the prison. The population at this time was 233 males and 50 females and with the increasing numbers it was necessary *"to impress prisoners with a stronger sense of the authority of the officers and materially promote the observance of due order and discipline"*.[42]

As the demands for prisons to reform prisoners increased, those working in prisons were expected to have high moral qualities. Certainly their characters were extolled as "far from a whining, canting class of men they should be manly and upright persons".[43] A Chaplain's view did not necessarily coincide with a prisoner's view who was at the receiving end of an officer's carrying out of the rules about hard labour. His control over the screw of the crank and treadmill to make the work easier or harder earned him the nickname of 'Screw' to generations of prisoners.

In the monotonous routine of a prison seeing the same faces day after day, the occasional visitor from the outside world would be a welcome relief. John Brown must have been one of these. He had been the prison chimney sweep for 18 years and during that time the changes in the prison had increased the number of chimneys. So in 1846 he asked for an increase in pay from £5 to £8 to sweep the prison's 100 chimneys four times a year. The Magistrates agreed.

These chimneys would have been part of the system that heated the cells by steam. Each cell was 10ft 5in x 6ft 10in x 10ft high, and had a large semi-circular aperture for the admission of light and air. It would be here under the Silent system that the time not working would be spent. Under the Separate system even more time would be spent as punitive work at the crank and oakum-picking would be done in cells.

Who were the people living out their days in the cells? Some were awaiting trial, some were in Knutsford for misdemeanours involving the Game and Bastardy Laws. Felons were more serious offenders and there were debtors who had offended Customs and Excise or the Revenue. There were men, women and juveniles. The records tell something of their story:

J.B., 18 years old, a prisoner confined here for the last year. He states that he was always a wild lad: he has very often spent the whole night in wandering about with his companions and without taking any rest in bed, has put on his working clothes and taken his regular turn of labour in the colliery. He was employed by women in the town to act as their protector, for which service he received many a pound, but the money did not him no good. His companions enticed him to join in robbing a post office, for

OFFICERS AND INMATES

Prison warders in their uniform. Uniforms were first issued under Governor George Gallop in October 1844. They were designed to "impress prisoners with a stronger sense of the authority of the officers and materially promote the observance of due order and discipline". (From the collection of Knutsford Historical Association)

which offence he was sentenced to 12 months' imprisonment. He can now read and write very well. He has a competent knowledge of his religious and moral duties and he intends, he says, to take heed to his ways in the future and abstain from all bad companions and other temptations to come.

Anne Jones, sentenced for burdening the township of Cuddington with a bastard child. She charges another prisoner William Hughes for getting her with child whilst he was employed in whitewashing the female part of the prison.

E.H., when 14 years of age, was driven out of her father's house by her stepmother. In a short time afterwards she fell into bad company, who enticed her from her native town and from that time to the present, a period of seven years, she has been pursuing the trade of prostitution. She now wishes to leave off that course of life and become a reformed character. 'Something,' *she says, 'tells me that I can have no peace and comfort while I continue on the town'. This girl has no home or friends, trade or occupation: no respectable housekeeper would receive her from this prison as a domestic servant and therefore I have recommended her for admission into the penitentiary.*[44]

Such a varied group of people no doubt found themselves prisoners for various reasons. Ignorance produced education as a possible cure. Idleness encouraged attempts to teach skills such as weaving and sewing. Drunkenness resulted in exhortation and books such as 'The Demon Drink'. Viciousness produced the ever-increasing emphasis on punishment.

The fact that prison of itself seemed not to work became evident to the Magistrates, at least in the case of juveniles. On April 4th 1846 they noted that in the year 1844-45 and so far in the current year, 145 orphans and illegitimate children had been inmates. They thought it *"well worthy the attention of the Court of Quarter Sessions to consider whether any plan can be devised to prevent the frequent return of that class of prisoners to the Gaol by instituting some careful watch over them for some period after their discharge".*[45] How the court responded is not recorded.

The Inspectors' 1837 Report gives the daily routine of prisoners:

"In Summer a bell rings a quarter before six so that the prisoners may have time to fold their bedding and the officers to assemble by six, when it again rings and the prisoners unlock. As the officer unlocks the door the prisoners walk out and stand opposite the cell until their bedclothes are examined and the order given to go below by the officer who unlocks. He then stands at the top of the stairs where he can observe them to the door of the day room. Another officer is there stationed to overlook them while they wash, for which purpose buckets are placed at intervals. Two men wash in each and go to their seats as they have done. By this time another passage is unlocked and proceed in like manner. All the felons go to one day room and the misdeamenants to another.

"Half past six – bell rings for work. When they leave the day room preceded by an officer who stands in the yard to observe them as they pass. Another remaining in the room until they have all left it.

"Half past eight – Breakfast bell rings, when prisoners leave their work in the same regular order and are marched to the mess room where the roll is called by an officer. Prisoners all face the officer and sit face to back. After breakfast prayers are read and they return to work at nine.

"'Twelve noon – Dinner bell rings when prisoners are conducted in the same way to dinner where they remain until twenty to one when they go to chapel and from thence to work which they leave at six go to supper and at half past six the bell rings for locking up, proceeding to their cells in the manner they left them.

"Prisoners' names are called over before each meal and grace said both before and after. On no account are prisoners left in the mess rooms without an officer. On Sundays prisoners remain in the day rooms or walk round the yard in single file during the intervals between chapel and meals overlooked by officers and are locked up as soon as they have had supper.

"A Wardsman is employed in each wing to clean and three of them walk the passages after locking up in order to report on any prisoner who call from his cell. When the watchman comes on duty he locks them up and unlocks them to perform the same duty an hour before the first bell rings. They cannot see or converse with each other, neither do they know who is locked in any cell as no prisoner sleeps two nights in the same wing. Each morning each prisoner's bedclothes are examined and once a week his clothing. When if any hole or tare is found not occasioned by regular wear, it is reported and the prisoner punished".[46]

This regimented routine was designed to achieve the ideal of the Silent system. Constant observation was designed to make communication impossible. Ideals come to grief on the rocks of reality as the Inspector had to recognise. "At the period of my visit the treadmill was not at work and the male prisoners were crowded together in the woolpicking room to a degree which must have rendered useless all attempts to prevent communication. I am quite aware that the former is profitless and the latter profitable employment. But this otherwise desirable object loses its value if only to be obtained by a sacrifice of the discipline. In the woolpicking room there were about 110 prisoners and so closely were they packed as even to embarrass each other in this simple employment. The overlooker states, 'It is impossible to prevent communication in the present crowded state of the room'".[47]

Among the population of prisoners there would inevitably be those who were especially difficult to manage. Those with a mental illness (described as lunatics in those days) were especially difficult to cope with. Governors were frequently pointing out the unsuitability of putting them in prison. Their supervision required additional officers but as in December 1842 often requests to have them moved to the asylum "were not responded to by The Secretary of State". These situations could develop tragically as occurred with one prisoner referred to as J.C. The Surgeon reported "death was occasioned by him attempting to destroy himself by cutting his throat... he was a man above the common rank of prisoners and depressed in spirits". The Chaplain added: *"I had frequent conversations with J.C. after he attempted to destroy himself. He said he had become weary of the world. But he made no complaint of any kind concerning the prison. On the contrary he expressed himself in grateful terms for the kind treatment he had received from everyone there"*.[48]

Obviously individuals of this kind continued to find themselves committed to Knutsford so often that the Visiting Magistrates produced a report on the matter to present to the meeting of The Sessions in August 1849. They begin with the general point, the frequency of commitments to the House of Correction of parties who at the time of their reception into prison are in an insane state and objects not of a prison but of an asylum. They give two examples, one is *"John Booth of Hyde now confined... for the fourth time. The charge against him is for an assault on his wife and when brought into the prison the account given of him by The Constable was most disgusting and it was borne out by the fact of his being at that time in so violent a state as to require the restraint of a straight waistcoat. He is now calm, but it is quite clear that when received into the prison he was not the object of punishment, but decidedly a person requiring different treatment to that afforded in a House of Correction."* They conclude: *"the named are evidently persons who ought not to have been committed to a House of Correction and the commitment of such persons on criminal charges is not only improper but of very questionable legality whilst it is converting the want of reason into a crime".*[49] The Visiting Magistrates hoped that either by a general circular to the magistracy or to the constables or by some other means the practice of committing insane persons to the House of Correction might be prevented. Sadly these hopes were not to be realised.

Each prisoner wore prison clothes – always designed to identify their status. In 1836 "the Convicted wore a particoloured suit of blue and yellow frieze, with cap and clogs. The Untried, a suit of light blue of the same materials, Misdemeanants sentenced to six months' imprisonment and upwards a suit of drab. The Females of all classes are clothed; a variety is made in the dress of each class."

In the early years prisoners slept in hammocks but by 1836 these had been changed to bedsteads of iron and wood, a pailliasse, two blankets and a rug with an extra one in winter. The straw stuffing of the pailliasse was changed to cocoa-nut fibre in 1844 and complaints about no heating in the cells were perhaps silenced by the newly built blocks being heated by steam.

The Visiting Magistrates received complaints from prisoners at their meeting. Those considered at the January meeting in 1844 give a flavour:

1. Complaint made that a prisoner's letter passed by the Governor for sending had been read by Turnkey. Justices pointed out that this was against the rules.

2. A prisoner for transportation complained of wrongful punishment. Justices said there was no foundation in the accusation.

3. A transport asked for the return of money taken from him on conviction.

4. A prisoner asked for help with expenses of travel on discharge. Given 5 shillings.

5. Complaint about distribution of bread. Dismissed.

6. Prisoner complained that the Constable had taken his money when he was arrested.

7. The individual who claimed his clothing had been damaged in the prison wash should have the item replaced by the Governor.

Unsatisfied by local arbitration, some like William Wright took it further to the Home Secretary. During April and May of 1844 he complained about the Governor, Surgeon and Chaplain as well as the Turnkeys. The Surgeon gave his opinion that *"Wright's proneness to complain is a symptom of monomania"*. After hearing his complaints about the washing of his flannel shirt the Magistrates concluded *"the complaint originated in a disposition to annoy the officers of the prison"*. When he moved on to complaining *"that he is getting worse meat and potatoes than others because of the discrimination of the turnkeys"* authority shows signs of being worn down. The Magistrates report: "Wright has been offered the privilege of choosing his own mess after the meals are set out". Maybe the fact that Wright had a high profile in the investigation into the treatment of Chartist prisoners had something to do with how his complaints were handled. They finally decided that the best way of dealing with this complainant extraordinaire was to move him to Chester for the last part of his sentence.

Chapter Seven

OUTSIDE AFFECTING 'INSIDE'

The House of Correction obviously had an effect on the life of the town – even if only at the level of the smoke from its chimneys causing a nuisance to the townsfolk. What happened in the town also made a difference to the gaol. In 1848 as part of the spread of railways in Cheshire a track was to cross the turnpike road opposite the prison by a 15ft excavation. The line of rails would be laid 50 yards from the prison wall. But the railway company intended to use the land up to the prison boundary, including that designated for the new Governor's house outside the prison. Such were the plans but they were dropped before the Magistrates could object and the house was built according to plan, although cost forced a change from stone to brick. Some years later the railway was built from Chelford to Knutsford and in June 1861 it was noted that a clause was to be inserted into the Parliamentary Bill to the effect 'it shall not be lawful for the Company to erect, construct have or use any Station, Manufactuary warehouse, Wharf, Yard, Stationary engine, Coke oven, Furnace, Workshop Engine Shed or any other building within 100 yards of The House of Correction'.[57]

Policy decisions in government on penal matters always had a potential power to change things in Knutsford Gaol. In the early part of 1847 the Secretary of State informed the Magistrates of their intention to suspend the transportation of male convicts to Van Dieman's Land. Those sentenced to transportation did not stay long in Knutsford before being transferred to Chester and then on to Millbank in London. From

KNUTSFORD PRISON – THE INSIDE STORY

This 1930s aerial photograph shows how near the railway is to the prison – a cause for concern in 1846 when plans for new lines, 50 yards from the prison wall, through Knutsford, threatened the construction of a new Governor's House. However the idea was dropped. When it was resurrected in 1861 by The London and North West Railway, a petition by the Magistrates resulted in building restrictions being imposed within 100 yards of the prison. (From the collection of Knutsford Historical Association)

there they embarked for Australia. Evidence before a Select Committee looking into conditions in gaols around the country includes that of a man of 31 who was "received into the Penitentiary on July 12th 1834 from Chester Gaol, having been tried at Knutsford Sessions. He was convicted of stealing potatoes (he states not more than a bushel) and sentenced to transportation for seven years".[58] It has been reckoned that between 1841-1850 some 16,000 convicts were sent to Van Dieman's Land and the practice was not stopped until 1853. But the suggestion of suspending transportation produced a report by the Governor and sent out over the signature of Egerton Leigh, the Chairman of the Visiting Magistrates. It gives a good description of the Gaol at the time.

There are five wards in use for Male Prisoners.

Wards 1 & 2 each contain 24 separate cells and Day rooms used for work. The prisoners are both adult and juveniles awaiting trial.

Wards 3 & 4 each contain 24 cells and Day rooms, Four of the cells are used for storage. Convicted male Misdemeanants are housed here.

Ward 5 contains 100 separate cells. 3 of these are used for storage the rest house convicted Felons.

During 1846 the largest number of Male prisoners at any one time was 222. These were accommodated in the following way:

Wards 1 & 2:   38 single cell and 18 three in cell
Wards 3 & 4:   35 single and 24 three in cell
Ward 5:   99 single.
In Solitary cells: 4
Hospital: 4

At the time of the report the population of Males was 224. These accommodated:

Ward 3:   66 three in cell
Ward 4:   42 three in cell. 8 single.
Ward 5:   97 single.

Building operations are causing the objectionable practice of three prisoners sharing one cell. When these are completed and Wards 1 & 2 are converted into one Ward for the separate confinement of

Juveniles and other offenders it is expected to increase the number of the cells from 48 to 72.

The discipline of the Gaol cannot be termed either Separate or Silent. Neither system can be carried out with all the current building activities. The Separate system does apply in Ward 5 as far as circumstances permit. In other parts of the Gaol work in classes at Woolpicking and other employments under the superintendence of officers of the prison, each class being kept separate from the other.

All this points to the obvious conclusion, *"There will not be in this Gaol any proper accommodation for the temporary imprisonment and employment of male convicts under sentence of transportation until the alterations now in progress are fully completed, so as to bring that part of the prison again into use and no arrangements can be made in the present state of the Gaol for the reformatory discipline of such prisoners. There are now eight convicts in this Gaol under sentence of transportation".*[59]

The year before transportation stopped there were reports on prisoners awaiting removal from Knutsford for transportation:

- Mary Jarvis, aged 54, her sentence of seven years was received for theft of a bed quilt, blanket, shawl and two flat irons. The Surgeon found her unfit due to loss of teeth and recommended clemency.
- Mary Brown was 31 and was sentenced to seven years for stealing a shawl and four sovereigns. She was unfit because of a syphylitic sore throat.
- Richard Turner at 62 was sentenced to seven years for obtaining sovereigns by false pretences – clemency was recommended.
- John Hardy was 40 and for stealing a turkey he received a seven-year sentence. As he was epileptic and violent the Magistrates recommended his removal "to another place".[60]

The policies adopted by other public institutions often had an effect on the prison. Constables who would bring their charges to the gaol at inconvenient times, such as late evening on a Sunday, were quickly put in their place by the Magistrates.

Their relationships with those who ran the workhouses were an ongoing problem. January 1846 found them in contact with Macclesfield and Stockport "to urge them to be cautious in taking in parties who on refusal to work after being inmates for a night are adjudged guilty of an imprisonable offence". Mr. Gallop, the Governor, reported that there were 44 prisoners in the prison for offences in the workhouse. The response of the Magistrates had a hint of sarcasm when suggesting a reason for this: *"either there is something wrong in the management of the establishment at Macclesfield and Stockport or there is an unusual amount of moral turpitude in the pauper population which the powers entrusted by law to officers of the Unions are insufficient to correct"*.[61] The sharpness of this obviously failed because November 1847 found them having to deal with 17 from Macclesfield workhouse where *"it appears to be the practice to relieve the wandering poor with a night's lodging and gruel night and morning for which the poor are required to do some labour. If they refuse they are sent to gaol at Knutsford"*. They have also been sent for *"tearing their clothes in the workhouse"*. These arrived at the gaol *"in coverings made from rice bags and no provision for clothes on discharge"*. All this caused the Magistrates to question the willingness of workhouse authorities to exercise discipline. *"The masters of Workhouses will no longer consider themselves to be discipline officers but will ease themselves of responsibility and their Unions of cost by procuring the commitment of every pauper who may presume to blow a whistle instead of being at the trouble to take the instrument out of his hand"*.[62] Their more incisive comment was *"some inmates of the workhouse wish to obtain the food given in prison in preference to that obtained in the workhouse"*.

As we have already seen the diet of those in prison was a difficult one to resolve. If it was harsh, prisoners' health could be adversely affected which would cause problems for Governors and Magistrates. If it was felt to be too generous then the principle of less-eligibility would be endangered and law-abiding citizens would sense an unfairness. Catering as they did for overlapping groups, it was inevitable that the conditions of the workhouses built under the Act of 1834 would frequently be compared with those in the prisons. Government recognised the problem in 1850 with the Grey Committee. Evidence received confirmed that offences were committed in workhouses in order to be sent to prison where the diet was better. Knutsford's diet was generally better than the basic laid down in Graham's Dietary of 1834. Indeed the fact that cocoa had been introduced would have aroused the anger of those who believed prison food should not compare favourably with that of free labourers or workhouse inmates and that "cocoa is both pleasant and costly enough to be considered a luxury". The problem continued to rumble on until the investigations of Lord Carnarvon and his Committee in 1863. A near neighbour of Knutsford, the Governor of Stafford Prison, gave evidence "that his prison was superior to the workhouse not only in diet, but also in bedding and general comfort and that workhouse inmates frequently committed offences in order to be imprisoned". With typical Victorian throughness the Governor of Taunton Gaol, William Oakley compared the diet of 46 workhouses with 50 county gaols and found that on the average of the gaols 267 ounces of solid food and 17 pints of liquid food was given each week to prisoners. In the workhouses the solid food given to paupers was 202 ounces and 16 pints of liquid food! The Carnarvon Committee's report was to lead to a new Prisons Act in 1865 which certainly had an effect on what was done in Knutsford Prison.

Chapter Eight

GETTING TOUGH ON CRIMINALS

As the century progressed people seemed to lose patience with the idea of reforming criminals. The fact that individuals returned to gaol again and again made them doubt that it was possible to change prisoners for the better. Religious convictions which had supported the idea came under attack in the 1850s and so more practical ideas were looked for. Society became tougher on those who fell on hard times, tending to hand out blame rather than help. Behind all this was a growing fear of 'the criminal classes' always threatening stability and contaminating the community. As they seemed to be on the increase, prison was a way of removing these bad apples from the lower classes before they could spread their malign influence. Transportation stopped after 1853, so unable to remove people they had to be contained safely. The response was to press for a policy of uniform repression, deterrence and retribution in the prisons.

Knutsford Magistrates were much exercised in keeping pace with rebuilding plans. In 1851 they gave a tender for four million bricks to James Potts of Auderley who would make them from clay in a field behind the gaol. At their meeting in January 1852 they noticed an increase in the number of people held awaiting trial. Their comment was *"the visiting justices are unable to account for this difference as work appears to be plentiful in the manufacturing districts and it would appear that some cause is in existence which produces crime of which the magistracy are not sufficiently informed. The attention of the police might be possibly directed with advantage to the cause of the increase in crime"*.[51]

Knutsford justices seem to be linking crime to the level of unemployment. Others, like the inspector visting Preston prison, concluded "drunkenness is the source of almost all crime and that destitution arising from want of employment acts far less prejudicially on the working classes than this monster vice".

Employing suitable officers for duty in the prison was a problem. It was found in 1853 that the average length of service was five years because there appeared to be little opportunity for advancement. Introducing an increase from 19s per week to 21s after three years did not satisfy. Indeed the officers presented a memorial about their pay, much to the annoyance of the Magistrates who saw in it *"too much the appearance of a combination"*.[52] They refused to consider it and criticised the Governor for assisting the officers and not warning them of what was happening. However when they did look into it the scale was revised. For the first two years it was 21s per week and then an increase of one shilling for each two years service up to eight years at 25s. Male officers living in the prison had a shilling deducted but were allowed coals and candles. Every nine months male officers were allowed a suit of uniform.

These officers were involved in a fire in the prison in February of 1853. Together with the Governor and prisoners *"many of who cheerfully turned out of their cells to work the pumps"* they put it out. It caused £20 worth of damage. The incident resulted in the Governor being authorised to purchase twelve gutta pecha buckets, "to be in readiness in the event of a recurrence of such a calamity". Arrangements were also made to insure the prison buildings against fire and the Magistrates ordered that ammunition belonging the The Cheshire Yeomanry and other public ammunition stored in the prison to be removed.

During this period we have already seen how the diet of prisoners became a matter of principle for the Magistrates. At the same time they needed to deal with the more basic problems of providing regular meals. Problems included the poor quality of the potatoes and their rise in price. The Governor's solution, supported by the Surgeon, was to substitute rice, cabbage and beans on five days of the week. Throughout there is the regular matter of contracts with local traders – a reference in 1857 is typical:

Beef without bone	5d per lb
Bread	6s 4d per 4lb loaf
Candles	6s 4d per doz
Coals	11s 6d per ton
New milk	2s 0d per doz quarts
Oatmeal	30s 0d per load
Molasses	8s 9d per cwt
Rice	8s 3d per cwt
Soap (hard)	33s 6d per cwt
Soap (soft)	18s 2d per firkin

During this year the House of Corrections was inspected and in the resulting report it was noted that "the provisions were of good quality and sufficient. The daily cost was 4¾d per head".

Pressure to make prison work more punishing was increasing, so in 1866 we find the Governor visiting Chester prison to inspect the shot drill ground.[53] Shot drill was a form of hard labour. It required the prisoner to stoop down without bending the knees, pick up a heavy cannon ball, bring it up slowly until level with the chest, take three steps to the right, replace it on the ground and then step back three paces to start all over

Shot drill. Prisoners had to move cannonballs from one pile to another. (Reproduced by kind permission of Inveraray Jail).

again. Warders shouted orders while prisoners, sweating profusely, moved cannon balls with precision from one pile to another. The Governor was impressed as was the committee of Magistrates set up to ensure that the provisions of the 1865 Act "be carried out with the greatest efficiency and economy in the County". By January of the next year decisions were made and a shed for shot-drill was ordered. It was noted that shot would be supplied "at cost" by the Secretary of State. So Knutsford now had the full punitive labour armoury of crank, treadmill and shot-drill. However, profitable labour had not been completely abandoned. The Magistrates' satisfaction in 1875 of knowing the average earnings per prisoner had gone up from £2 16s 5d to £2 19s 0d would have helped balance the criticism of the Prison Inspector. His general satisfaction had an exception: *"he found a number of prisoners working together in the mat-room instead of separately"*.[54]

There were two ominous notes in this year. In January and October there were records of deaths in the previous quarter. One was from apoplexy, one from inflammation of the lungs, two from bronchitis and one from exhaustion. How far the exhaustion was due to hard labour is uncertain but combined with a more rigorous diet there was an obvious danger. The local contracts for cocoa, molasses, peas and potatoes were not renewed. Changes to the diet were reported to "have worked well" when they were introduced in 1866 subject to Home Office approval. However the diet became a cause of disagreement between Governor and Surgeon. Should it be applied in the sick wards? Obviously the dispute became heated because both were required to apologise in the Magistrates' presence for *"all hasty personal explosions that had been uttered by one to the other"*.[55] But the Magistrates ordered that the diet for the prison should also apply to the sick. Presumably in order to monitor any easing of its strictness on medical grounds, the Surgeon was required to present his journal to the Governor every day.

We have already seen how some medical opinion believed diet not only was important for physical wellbeing but also for

maintaining prisoners' spirits. The recording of three apparent suicides in the years 1872-1874 highlights this:
- In December 1872 Mary Burke, a female prisoner, had been found strangled by her apron. She had been discharged on November 5th and then committed again for vagrancy. She appeared to be in good health.
- On July 25th 1873 John Whitby hanged himself whilst in a fit of temporary insanity.
- In February 1874 John Dipping, a prisoner, hanged himself. The verdict at the Coroner's inquest was an open one, the jury not finding whether the death was accidental or otherwise.

The working out of the 1865 Act obviously involved the Magistrates in considerable effort. Imagine their annoyance when, at the end of 1867, the Secretary of State for the Home Office wrote to them suggesting they had made little provision for its implementation. They ordered the Governor to write reporting the building alterations and their expectation of having an extra 91 cells by the summer of 1868. He should also point out their introduction of shot-drill.

There were also new ways of discovering who among the newly arrived had previous convictions. Photography was introduced in the Habitual Criminals Act of 1869. This required certain classes of criminals to be photographed and copies sent to the Commissioner of Police for the Metropolis. The Governor was ordered to obey the Act *"at as little expense to the County as possible"*. As always there was a need for accommodation and eventually a small building used as a W.C. was replaced by one suitable for the photographing of prisoners.

The revolutionary Fenians were serious criminals, so much so that in 1866 Habeas Corpus was suspended when a rising was feared. Knutsford Magistrates were concerned enough to request a stand of arms for the House of Correction and did receive twenty revolvers. In 1868 concern was still in the air and in January the Governor was required to get an estimate for a large alarm bell and to issue each officer with a railway whistle. Tension obviously mounted for a special meeting was held at ten in the evening on January 5th. Information had been received that a Fenian attack on the prison was expected. Special constables were sworn in. Meetings were held on Monday and Tuesday and all precautions thought necessary were taken. During all this the Governor was in London discovering that a suitable alarm bell would cost £31 18s 8d. Although nothing more was heard of that proposed attack, it was decided in September to make plans, with the help of the military, to secure the prison from external attack.

The Fenians were Irish nationalists, but it was the influx of Irish immigrants into the North West that encouraged pressure to give recognition to the work of Roman Catholic priests among prisoners. The Knutsford Magistrates considered they were doing all that was necessary. Way back in 1852 they had refused to agree to Father O'Reilly's request that all R.C. inmates should be gathered together for instruction. While *"anxious to construe the rules in as liberal a spirit as possible"* they felt his request *"was inconsistent with the classsification of prison"*.[56] In 1863 the Prison Ministers Act allowed Magistrates to appoint and pay ministers not of the Established Church. When Fr. Hugh Lynch of Knutsford asked that it should be implemented he was told *"the facilities already for intercourse between priest and R.C. prisoners were sufficient"*. This view was supported by the fact that over the past four years less than a quarter of the total receptions – 8,434 – were R.C. Of these 1,835 prisoners, a third were doing sentences of less than one month. Although the Act required Roman Catholic prisoners to ask especially to see the R.C. priest, the Knutsford Governor regularly informed all Roman Catholic prisoners of the priest's visit each month. In the Magistrates' view this went beyond what was required of them. They also pointed out that nearly all R.C.s attended the daily chapel services and they rarely asked to see their priest even when sick. As from 1866 all new arrivals in the prison would be asked *"to what religious persuasion they belong"*, the R.C. priest could visit each Sunday afternoon and four dozen copies of the Roman Catholic Prayer Book and Bible were ordered for his use. The following year the Magistrates agreed to pay the R.C. Chaplain £40 per year but they did not agree to his request for a separate R.C. place of worship.

The month before this happened, September 1868, the Church of England Chaplain resigned his post after 25 years in the prison. It appears that his "stomach derangement and suppressed gout", because of which he had been given two months leave of absence, must have been the reason. When the advertisement for the position was published, a salary of £250 was offered to candidates who were over thirty years old. There was a good response and 48 candidates sent applications and testimonials. The short-list of four included men from Norfolk, Nottingham and Scarborough. William Truss from Wolverhampton was chosen and he came having experience of Manchester City Gaol.

Chapter Nine

POWER TO THE CENTRE

The story of the development of prisons shows the tendency to centralise. Individual prisons had gone their own way until Prison Inspectors brought some guidance and advice from the centre. This soon became directives and instruction couched in respectful language to maintain good relations with the local Magistrates who could be difficult if their position seemed threatened. As we have seen these local Magistrates were prepared to give of their time and interest. At the same time they were cautious in spending the ratepayers' money. However the desire at the centre to control, linked with the prospect of reducing costs, was irresistible and in April of 1876 Knutsford received a copy of the new Prisons Bill which proposed centralising all the prisons under a Prisons Commission. Their first reaction appears to have been to express *"the need to safeguard the County's position"*.[63]

Sadly it was not George Gallop who was to oversee this transfer of power. In January he resigned for health reasons and died the following month. It was Captain Henry Talbot Price, the new Governor, who in September 1877 escorted Sir Edmund Du Cane and Admiral Hornby around the prison. These were two of the Commissioners appointed by the 1877 Prisons Act. Sir Edmund became the Chairman of the Commission and was known to want "a clean, mean and lean prison service". He would have been glad to learn on his visit that the average cost per week per prisoner for provisions was 3s and that the new Governor had decided to change to plank beds at a cost of 5s per bed.

In 1878 we begin to see how the new Act would affect Knutsford. On April 15th the records show a change from Knutsford House of Correction to Her Majesty's Prison Knutsford. The subjects discussed become less directly about the details of life within the prison. Instead they are letters handing down decisions on contracts, accounts, salaries and inspections. Even stationery and uniforms are matters for central decision rather than local initiative. The Agenda Book shows how their meetings assumed a pattern: examine the Books of Officers of the Prison; Prisoners Aid Grants; sign Bills and visit prison. This last item is almost a laying down of a marker of intent to hang on to an involvement with the day to day life of the prisoners.

An early problem was over the Sessions House which had not been taken over, in total, by the Prison Commission as it was part of the Courts system. Yet physically it was part of the prison boundary. Who was to keep it clean? An early suggestion that officers of the prison should maintain it for a charge came to nothing when the Governor's charge was thought excessive. The Clerk to the Justices was ordered to find a local cleaner but this became difficult when the Prison Commissioners did not like the idea of a caretaker living on the premises so near to the prison. What was County property and what was Prison Commissioners' occupied much time and effort. When the County wanted to improve the sanitary arrangements in the Sessions House they found they were hindered by not having access to parts controlled by the Commissioners. In December 1881 there is a letter from the Commissioners about who owned a gas meter in the Sessions House. Was it theirs or the County's? Someone somewhere decided it was Government property![64] The following year the Visiting Justices record their position on the ongoing dispute. "The Visiting Committee are of the opinion that such portions of the building as have hitherto been used for a magisterial and judicial proceeding and also part of the cellarage beneath the Magistrates' room belong to the County. Such building and

KNUTSFORD PRISON – THE INSIDE STORY

The Prison in the early 1900s. It is easy to see how the Sessions House is part of the prison's boundary wall - something which was to cause problems when deciding what was the responsibility of The Prison Commission and what the County should be responsible for.
(From the collection of the Knutsford Historical Association)

rooms as are used and are necessary for the containment of prisoners or for the abode and use of officers and the prisoners belong to the Prison Commissioners Rooms in the Court House currently used by the Prison Commissioners: Porter's Lodge, Rooms used to house two prison officers and families, a cellar under the Magistrates' room." Eventually at a meeting with representatives from London it was agreed that the Commission would hand over the Porter's Lodge and the accommodation for two officers. The County would pay the cost of erecting two new officer's quarters on prison land on the South side of the prison, provided that prison labour and old materials would be used as far as possible. In May 1882 the Governor of the prison was asked to "deliver over" the Union Jack flag belonging to the Court House and in June the Prison Commissioners instructed the Governor to comply. Even this did not draw a line under the dispute. When the County wished to reglaze the window of the Magistrates' room, the Commissioners claimed responsibility for half of the inner wall of the Court House as the boundary of the prison. The Magistrates, unwilling to give any acknowledgement to this, returned their cheque for half the cost of the reglazing to the Governor of the prison.[65]

Of course while all this was going on the Prison Commission were managing the routines of the prison. Indeed very soon after taking over they started a major building programme. Their first report in 1879 describes how, "On 9th April 1878 No. 2 Wing of the prison was pulled down. This work involved much care to prevent accidents, masses of stone weighing one ton and upwards having to be lowered down and the excavation commenced necessary for the erection of a new cook house and bakery which it was decided upon to build. This building with chimney stack 60ft high was erected almost entirely by prison labour, one paid bricklayer being called in to assist and it took about six months to complete. It was fitted with new boilers and the cooking apparatus was arranged in such a manner as to carry out the new dietary system recently introduced." The new dietary was accordingly commenced in Febrnary 1879 and bread for the first time manufactured on the premises on April 1st 1879.

But prisoners could not live by bread alone and the regime advocated by Du Cane soon came in for criticism. General deterrence was his aim and he claimed that punishment was inflicted "much more for the purposes of deterring from crime the enormous number of possible criminals rather then the effect on the criminal himself". So ideas of reforming the individual prisoner were put to one side and the terror of the general harshness of the routine emphasised. Any work that was productive was suspect as this might reduce its ability to punish. Much of the effect of all this was hidden behind the high walls of the prisons. Gradually however details of what was happening emerged. Reductions in the costs of imprisonment, which had been promised, were not forthcoming. The numbers of those being reconvicted increased, suggesting that people were not being deterred, despite the harshness. In 1894 the press became interested and a series of articles in *The Daily Chronicle* helped to influence public opinion. Confidence in the Prison Commissioners was undermined and eventually a Departmental Committee under Hubert Gladstone was set up. Although it tried to reconcile the old conflict between deterrence and reform the task proved impossible. The needs of individual prisoners and the requirements of the prison system could not be satisfied easily. There was a Departmental Committee on Education in 1896 at which William Truss the Knutsford Chaplain gave evidence.[66] He spoke of the difficulty of one schoolmaster being available for 370 male prisoners and how meeting together for classes was impossible. From his description of the various duties expected from the teacher only half an hour each day could have been spent in actual teaching. The Committee in its recommendations recognised the problem. "The principle which underlines imprisonment… is separation; and this principle cannot be overlooked in any recommendation for moral improvement. All who have had

The Sessions House (From the collection of the Knutsford Historical Association)

experience of crime and criminals agree as to the terrible evils resulting from the injudicious association of prisoners". These conflicts were not to be reconciled during the period Knutsford was part of the prison system. Indeed they still tax the prison manager's ingenuity. [67]

After 1886 when Chester Castle became a military prison, Knutsford became the prison where executions took place. The scaffold was transported and set up in a detached building within the walls, a few yards from the entrance lodge and about fifty yards from the condemned cell. Of course public executions had been abolished in 1868. There had often been scenes of public disorder and drunkenness – more like a fairground than the serious occasion meant to deter and warn. One of the Chaplains attending the execution of a young woman in Chester wrote to the Magistrates complaining of how the press had intruded on the woman's last moments. Horatio Walpole, twice Home Secretary, wrote that "execution scenes had become so demoralising that instead of its having a good effect, it has the tendency rather to brutalise the public mind than to deter the criminal class from committing crime".

Once the management of prisons became centralised in the

Prison Commission the government was concerned that nothing should happen to cause it embarrassment. The same year that responsibility for carrying out executions passed from Chester to Knutsford, a Departmental Committee of Enquiry into the Execution of the Death Penalty was set up. It investigated the gruesome details necessary to ensure it was done speedily and with appropriate efficiency. The "mechanics of the drop" as they described it was examined by doctors and engineers to avoid unseemly incidents. The appointment of the executioner, which had varied around the country, was looked into. Individuals given the job had sometimes behaved in ways that embarrassed the authorities. It was decided that the man appointed should remain in the prison all the time he was in town rather than be free to go the rounds of the local public houses feeding the gossip which inevitably surrounded executions.

The first execution at Knutsford was of Owen McGill, found guilty of the murder of his wife. On February 22nd 1887 the minute bell of the Parish church tolled from 7.45am until 8.00am when he was executed. In the same year on August 16th, Thomas Bevan, an iron moulder working at Crewe, went to his death for killing Sarah Griffith. The Davis brothers were convicted of the murder of their father in 1890. Robert was 20 and his younger brother George was 16. The trial revealed that their father had been a bully and a tyrant. In a rather confused incident on his way home from his clothier's shop in Crewe, accompanied by George, he was killed. Both sons were accused and convicted. However George was reprieved because of his age but on February 8th Robert was executed. On August 22nd Felix Spicer followed him, convicted of the murder of his two young sons.

As can be imagined there was intense interest centred on the prison when it was known that someone was in the condemned cell. On August 2nd 1905, *The Guardian* reported, "The High Sheriff of the County, Mr. Hornby Lewis has been notified of the date of the execution of William Alfred Hancocks, aged 58 of Birkenhead who was sentenced at the present Chester Azzize for the murder of his 18-year-old daughter, which is Wednesday August 8th at 8.00am. Hancock, who is in Knutsford gaol, was recommended to mercy by the jury, but as far as can be gathered, no efforts are being made to petition the Home Secretary for a reprieve. The condemned man holds out little hope of a commutation of the sentence and is preparing for the end. He has not been visited by relative or friend." In its next edition it reports on a petition organised in Birkenhead where Hancocks lived and his daughter was killed. Despite several thousands going to sign at the newspaper office, among whom were prominent citizens, a reprieve was not given. The execution was carried out by Billington, the premier hangman. Surprisingly *The Guardian* reported in its August 2nd edition that Billington was in Knutsford prison "having been transferred from Strangeways. He is undergoing a month's imprisonment for neglecting to support his wife." The following year Edward Hartigan was executed on August 7th for murdering his wife while in a drunken rage.

It is difficult for us to imagine how executions affected the public mood. James Philipps was due to go to his death on November 12th 1908. The day before the local newspaper reported the last visit of his parents and how two of his friends, from the Salt Union where he had worked, managed to persuade the Governor to allow them to visit the condemned man. The emotional content of their conversation was reported as was the fact that James Philipps attended the Church Service on the Sunday before the execution. He appeared to listen carefully to the Chaplain's sermon on an appropriate text. The Vicar of Over, where the condemned had lived, drew a discreet veil over his last visit. On the Sunday following, November 13th, he did, according to *The Guardian*, preach to a crowded congregation on the text "Thou shall not delay" incorporating into his sermon a last letter written by James urging his friends and neighbours not to delay in changing their lives to follow the better way. A letter from the Prison Chaplain, who had been with him, was also read out and gave an insight into how executions affected those closely involved in carrying them out. "Thank God it is all over. James died not only repentant but full of sure and certain hope. He displayed Christian bravery at the last. I was with him for nearly an hour the morning before the execution and it cheered me to see his confidence. It was an awful thing to see a young life go down and it is an awful lesson to the careless and indolent".

In total nine executions took place in Knutsford.

Chapter Nine

BEING LOCAL IS USEFUL

Control from the centre was obviously a frustration for local Magistrates who were used to command and felt a responsibility in local affairs. Being mere recipients of decisions reached by others was not what they were used to. The fact that they were late in returning the required annual report of their activities and questioned the need for an annual report suggests some resistance and doubt. However they could and did involve themselves in individual cases and made it clear that they felt their immediate involvement in matters of discipline could be a better way of dealing with difficult individual prisoners.

John Graham was released from Knutsford in 1898. A few days after discharge he travelled to Govanhall in Glasgow. His friends and family were shocked when they saw him and when he died a few days later complaints were made to the Prison Commissioners who ordered an inquiry at Knutsford. A Glasgow doctor, Dr. Burgess, who saw him and examined him before he died, accused the prison authorities of neglect and of sending him out suffering from pulmonary tuberculosis. To the Knutsford enquiry came Major Clayton, a Prison Commission official, Captain Pennethorne who had been Governor at the time of Graham's imprisonment and a Dr. Harris, an authority on diseases of the chest. The enquiry took a dim view of Dr. Burgess's failure to attend because of his holiday arrangements despite their willingness to reimburse all his expenses. The prisoner's friends spoke of "not recognising John Graham" he was so ill and of his constant cough and spitting of blood. They stated that he had made unfavourable comments on the quality and quantities of the prison food and had complained that the prison doctor had been lax in his attention and care. Prison officials, including warders and the Chaplain, said Graham had never made any complaint to them despite their frequent conversations with him. The Doctor, Dr. Fennell, described the prisoner's diet. "He was getting a pound and a half of bread and besides that, on two days a week he was getting a pint of good soup made from fresh meat and vegetables. On another day he would have potatoes, another day bacon and on another day suet puddings. And also a pint of milk every day". The chest specialist concluded: "Such a condition as that described by Dr. Burgess could not possibly have existed here in the face of the evidence. He must have got worse after he had left here and that would make the signs all the more distinct". In the face of this evidence and despite the strong insistence of John Graham's friends and relations, the Chairman of the Visiting Magistrates concluded: "I think we must attach weight to what the officials have said. It was known that he (John Graham) wanted attention and he was getting it and all the evidence we have goes to say that they would have taken care of him if they had thought him really ill. I don't see in the evidence anything to justify the charge of negligence and carelessness against the officials". [68]

Before being tempted to think this was a matter of the authorities supporting their officials against complaints from mere members of the public, consider the case of John Lenham in 1905. The prisoner came to Knutsford from Liverpool. He spoke of being falsely accused and the impossibility of him having been where the crime had been committed. His alibi had not been accepted. His petition to the Home Secretary to look into the matter ended in failure. The Knutsford Visiting Magistrates took up the matter, requesting their clerk to investigate. While this was happening Lenham was released after an investigation by the Liverpool police. The Magistrates claimed their enquiries had prompted the fresh findings of the police but this was denied by the Home Office who had refused to divulge the nature of the police investigations claiming they were confidential. Later the Visiting Magistrates were presented with a bill for £10 2s 7d by the solicitor who had enquired into John Lenham's case. When they attempted to recover these costs from public funds they were met with a refusal from the Prison Commission. They had not authorised the Visiting Committee to act in this way and in their view it was no part of the duties of Visiting Committees to investigate the guilt or otherwise of individual prisoners. The Home Office was appealed to and they concluded "after careful consideration of all the facts, they do not think the Visiting Committee make out a reasonable case for reimbursements out of public funds". Unsatisfied by this they sought the help of M.P.s to raise the matter in Parliament. By this time the amount of money had become irrelevant and the principle of the authority of the Visiting Committee was the important matter at stake. On 31st July 1906 a letter was received from Herbert Samuel of the Home Office which brought the dispute to an end. He wrote "the release of the prisoner was ordered, not on the evidence of an alibi put forward by Mr. Caldecott (Clerk to the Visiting Committee) but on account of other circumstances brought to the notice of Mr. Akers-Douglas by the police (this was the confidential police information and not available to the Magistrates)." With nothing else that they could do the Visiting Committee finally agreed in July 1907 that the costs involved should be divided equally between the members. The records contain the notes which accompanied the 12s 6d each magistrate contributed. The comment Lord Egerton wrote accompanying his cheque probably tells us how they all felt. He believed they were "being mulched in exercise of their duties" and the Home Office "has hardly done justice to their excellent intentions in dealing with a case where there has been some miscarriage of justice".[69]

If this concern for the individual developed into a principled stand for the authority of the Visiting Magistrates, the question of corporal punishment was from the start an attempt to assert their powers. Visiting Magistrates had always been involved in the punishment of prisoners who offended against prison rules. The infliction of corporal punishment had always required their involvement. When the Act of 1898 restricted corporal punishment to the gravest offences of violence it also required the evidence of the case to be forwarded to the Secretary of State for him to confirm the sentence before it was carried out. Many Visiting Committees felt strongly about this and Knutsford received requests to give support in trying to bring about changes. Strong feelings were expressed from Carmarthen under the Chairmanship of Lt. General J. Hills-Johnes G.C.B., V.C. "We must decline to be treated as inhuman nonentities, not fit to be trusted with the power of directing corporal punishment, even in cases of flagrant insubordination and we cannot but believe that you will have great difficulty in finding Magistrates willing to accept a position of such restricted authority". In November 1900 at Knutsford a sentence of 24 strokes of the 'cat' was remitted because the doctor thought the delay of punishment while awaiting the Secretary of State's confirmation, might induce suicide or a total collapse of the prisoner's health. Joynson, the Chairman of the Visiting Committee, believed that if corporal punishment was to be inflicted it should be done immediately and not delayed by a wait for confirmation from London. Seeing a newspaper account of a prisoner at Winson Green Gaol Birmingham collapsing under the 'cat', he wrote to the Visiting Committee there for more details. As ever the press reports were inaccurate. What had happened was that the doctor present, believing the prisoner "appeared likely to faint" stopped the punishment after eight strokes of an 18-stroke sentence. However the chairman wrote "I fully agree with you that it should be carried out at once. The anxiety caused by the long waiting to know the worst, is I consider little less than needless cruelty and on a former occasion, where a difference of opinion as to the number of strokes, necessitated some ten days correspondence'. Finally he says he is willing to join with other Visiting

Committees in applying pressure on the Prison Commission and Government.

The next year Knutsford's Visiting Committee learned of the failure to change the Government's view. Despite a deputation to the Home Secretary, J. Courtney Lord of Winson Green concluded that as Parliament was against the view of the Visiting Committees they would not support the Home Secretary's attempt to restore the Magistrates' powers. In any event the current Chairman of The Prison Commission, Ruggles-Brise "is one of the so called humanitarian types who do not believe in corporal punishment and will do all he can do to stop it". Prior to this the Knutsford Magistrates had decided against a sentence of corporal punishment in a case of violence to another prisoner because they believed it would not be confirmed. The Home Office refused to accept this suggestion that they did not confirm sentences handed down by Magistrates. They pointed out that during the year 1900 there were about 47 prisoners ordered to be flogged or birched and in all except four instances the order was confirmed. In a letter a few days later on April 27th the Home Secretary pointed out that the idea that the Winson Green prisoner fainted because of the anxiety built up by a long wait before his sentence was confirmed was false. The Visiting Committee's letter reporting the sentence was answered the next day and confirmed. Despite this Joynson wrote a final letter on July 14th 1901: "We had hoped to enlist your sympathy and secure your co-operation in obtaining some modification of an Act which so materially, though unintentionally, aggravates a prisoner's punishment and we must regret to find from your letter that we have failed in our object".

Complying with the Prison Commission's instructions, they received on March 20th 1902 the confirmation of 18 strokes of the birch rod on Frank Holland. However in the country's prisons the unhappiness of the Magistrates was still present and surfaced again with a memorial of the Visiting Committee of H.M.P. Liverpool. They claimed that the removal of the power to order corporal punishment had had a severe adverse effect on prison discipline. Prisoners knowing of the limitations on the Magistrates took advantage. Magistrates' powers should be restored. Knutsford sent its support adding the suggestion: "We are of the opinion that if the discretion formerly enjoyed by the Visiting Committee cannot be restored to them in its entirety, some limitation might be put which would be a satisfactory solution of the question. We would suggest that a Visiting Committee should have full discretion to use the birch, say up to 12 or 18 strokes: better still 24, but that the severer punishment – by the cat, must first be sanctioned by the Home Secretary". The saga continued with the Magistrates having to get central confirmation of any sentence. This was done in November 1904 when their decision that John Spenser should receive 30 strokes of the birch was confirmed. However they had not completely set their resistance to rest. The following month their wish that any confirmation should be sent by return of post was deemed not possible. The following year they were reminded of their limitations when their sentence of 36 lashes with the 'cat' was reduced to 24, because the offence was not of the most serious nature and it was rare that the maximum sentence was ever inflicted.[70]

Depending on your point of view these were battles of principle or attempts to show that local opinion must be considered. While they were going on the Magistrates involved themselves in the basic requirements needed to keep the prison running. Their concern in 1901 about a shortage of officers was met with a Prison Commission letter informing them that the Governor had been instructed to employ temporary officers so long as the male population exceeded 300. A shortage of trained officers prevented them doing more. The discipline of Hard Labour was still urged on them and they were directed that those prisoners who were sentenced to one month or less (these made up 68% of the total prison population) should be more severely supervised as they picked oakum and be subject to a more rigorous and uniform system. Their complaint about

> Any further communication on the subject of this letter should be addressed to—
> THE UNDER SECRETARY OF STATE,
> HOME OFFICE,
> LONDON, S.W.
> and the following number quoted—
> 148,969/16.

HOME OFFICE,
WHITEHALL

30th September, 1915.

Sir,

    I am directed by the Secretary of State to say, for the information of the Visiting Committee, that in compliance with the request of the Army Council he has decided to place at their disposal H.M.Prison, Knutsford, for temporary use as a Detention Barrack. The present population of the Prison is very low and the military authorities are experiencing great difficulty in finding accommodation for soldiers sentenced to detention for military offences. The Secretary of State has therefore arranged for the committal to other Prisons of prisoners who are at present sent to Knutsford. The change will take effect on the 11th proximo.

          I am,

            Sir,

              Your obedient Servant,

                HBSimpson

The Clerk to the
    Visiting Committee,
        H. M. Prison,
            Knutsford.

Letter from The Home Office saying the prison buildings were to be transferred to the Army Council as a "detention barrack".
(Cheshire and Chester Archives and Local Studies)

the quality of the bread given to prisoners was taken up and the contractor was changed. However in the same year, 1905, their complaint that Knutsford was being used as a dumping ground for badly behaved prisoners from Liverpool was dismissed as "not well founded".

The Annual Reports of the Visiting Committee give an insight into their other activities. They were usually full of praise for the Governor and his dealings with both officers and prisoners. Few instances of violence indicated to them a positive atmosphere in the prison. R.H. Joynson, their Chairman in 1904, refers to their usual monthly meetings when every part of the prison was visited and every prisoner asked whether he or she had any complaint to make. He applauded "the various reformatory agencies now at work in the prison. The Chaplain (Revd. W. Truss) and the R.C. Priest (Father Roche) have been assiduous in their ministrations to the prisoners which we believe have been well received. The work done by the two Lady Visitors, Miss Wright and Miss Winstanley is valued. They have been unceasing in their efforts in influencing women for good and it is satisfactory to record, with the best results in more than a few cases. The Church Army is seen as a powerful and most successful agency for good. One of its officers, a Captain Andrews, has recently concluded a 14 days mission in the goal and there is every reason to believe the good results will be deep and lasting. The Visiting Committee would gladly welcome two missions a year instead of the one as at present".[71]

The 1907 Annual Report "notes another moral agency for the reclamation of prisoners has been adopted in the gaol as in many others, namely the forming of a subcommittee to organise and carry out what is known as the Borstal System for dealing with juvenile adults. The Visiting Committee believed that if the system can only be carried out, as it ought to be, it will prove the most effectual means yet adopted, for the reformation of those who would otherwise form part of the criminal population of the country'.[72]

It is clear that the Borstal system did not turn out to be the solution to juvenile crime, despite the likes of Mr Charles Russell who worked among the juvenile adult prisoners in Manchester and assisted Knutsford's Governor. In 1913 his Visiting Committee was invited to support the Magistrates of Lewes prison who were pressing for legislation allowing males up to 21 years to be birched. They claimed "from their own observation of the numbers of boys convicted and committed to prison, many of whom they felt sure, need never have been sent there... had they had a good whipping when first they began to get into trouble".

However by this time the numbers of women being sent to Knutsford had been falling drastically. The courts at Chester, Runcorn and Stockport sent the largest number and it was cheaper to send the convicted to Liverpool and Manchester. Male numbers were reduced too and on 30th September 1915 the Visiting Committee received the letter informing them that the prison buildings were to be transferred to the Army Council as a Detention Barracks.

The records contain a letter from an ex-prisoner A.A. Cannon, dated 16th January 1908, who lived in Aberdeen. He writes to the Chairman of Knutsford's Visiting Committee complaining about his treatment in Stafford prison where he had been sent from Knutsford. His letter contains these two sentences. "I would say that it is my personal opinion that the whole of the prison staff takes its cue from the Governor. At Knutsford every warder I saw treated prisoners humanely and with consideration, while the Governor spoke to prisoners as one gentleman would speak to another".[83] John Howard in his book "The State of the Prisons" published in Warrington in 1777 wrote: "The first care must be to find a good man for a gaoler. One who is honest, active and humane".

The Prison Act of 1823, just after Knutsford Gaol opened its doors, required the Magistrates to organise the prison on John Howard's principles. How many of those who were sentenced to live in the building on the triangle of land bounded by Toft, Stanley and Bexton Roads would say they had succeeded?

APPENDIX

Gaol Visiting Register September 1820 — September 1915

The Gaol Visiting Register records the visits of Magistrates from September 1820 until September 1915. These visits were made by a group of Magistrates or by individuals. The entries are signed and so we discover who were the local magnates: Egerton, Legh, Mainwaring, Davenport and Trafford are the most frequent signatories. Sometimes we read of how they intervened in particular situations and issued instructions. Sometimes, more especially as authority passed to the central Prison Commission, their visits were more routine and they simply state 'found everything clean and in order'.

1820 September 19th
A complaint was made of the Bread being short by weight which appeared on examination to be well founded. It was therefore ordered that the Baker having thus broken his contract be dismissed. Mr D...... be ordered to make a fresh appointment with another baker and the bread be in future weighed previous to the delivery to the prisoners.

Randle, Wibraham, Egerton

1821 September
We the undersigned having investigated charges by a prisoner of the name of Thomas Mellor against William Lamb, Turnkey, for permitting spiritous liquor to be introduced into the gaol at Knutsford.... William Lamb is a improper person to be employed as a Turnkey of the Gaol and ought forthwith to be discharged. Ordered that the Gaoler shall on no account employ any prisoner to go on errands or any other business out of the walls of the prison.

Trafford

APPENDIX

1822 September 20th
We the undersigned, Visiting Magistrates, having taken into consideration a proposal from the Committee of Ladies interesting themselves in providing Labour and Instructions for the Female Prisoners.... that a Matron be appointed to superintend the female prisoners. Ordered that the Governor do admit the members of the Ladies Committee between eight and five of the clock.

Egerton Leigh, Trafford, Egerton

1823 September 11th
It appears that the prisoners at work on the treadmill are allowed to talk together. At Gloucester they are prohibited (and a guard constantly employed to prevent them so doing). When at once acts as an increase of punishment and a preventative of evil communication. At Gloucester the relief (i.e. the five persons at rest) are made to walk about until called into active duty.

Davenport

1825 June 13
Mr. Hudson reported that John White and William Wardle attempted to escape on Monday.... thro' the main drain. I have permitted the irons to be taken off, in consequence of their promise of future good behaviour. I have likewise ordered John Stevens to be released from his irons.

1827 July 6th
Visited the gaol at the request of Mr. Christmas having stated 37 prisoners convicted and sentenced to hard labour being in a very refractory state and refusing to work. We have accordingly.... on diligent inquiry found the complaint to be very correct and serious and have therefore sentenced Jock Whitely and William Govan to receive 6 dozen lashes each and the remainder of the prisoners to be held in solitary confinement until Monday next and kept on bread and water only.

1827 December 29th
Visited the gaol this day. - The prisoners were reported to be regular in their conduct. It is reported to me that two prisoners lately admitted are not right in the head. One of whom is in for felony.

1843 December 19th
Mr. Mainwaring and myself attended the gaol to hear certain complaints made by Stephen, Brannon-Lee and Hodson. The two former against the Surgeon. The two latter with regard to the potatoes. We enquired carefully into the same and found all to be frivolous and groundless. We inspected the provisions at Dinnertime and found them excellent and admitted to be so by the prisoners.

Egerton Leigh

1843 December 30th
Visited the gaol and inspected the Beef – 500lbs – which I (The Governor and Taskmaster being present) considered of excellent quality.

Mainwaring

1845 October 9th
Inspected the gaol with satisfaction as regards it maintenance, but I regret finding the prisoners are not more separate and left exposed to contamination.

Davenport

1845 October 25th
Complaints were made by several convicted felons that they were kept too long at work. On enquiry it appears that none are worked more than 9 hours and 40 minutes which is within the time limited by Act of Parliament and in accordance with the existing gaol rules. The prison clean and orderly.

APPENDIX

1847 August 7th
Visited the Gaol found the building advancing very satisfactory and in all good order, but too full.
Legh, Townshend, Mainwaring

1848 April 22nd
Refused permission to the Debtors to have a newspaper in the Gaol.

1848 October 16th
I have visited the County Prison at Knutsford this day and have been much pleased with the progress made in the adoption of the Separate System and the intelligence and interest in his work exhibited by Mr Gallop, the Governor, by whom I was accompanied. The Dietary of this and other County prisons appears to me to form a <u>great inducement to crime</u> and to require the constant attention of the Magistrates and Government of this country.
A Visiting Magistrate of the Devon County Prisons

1852 October 19th
Visited the gaol and was much satisfied by the inspection of all its arrangements and particularly the perfect system of the Bookkeeping.

1857 August 21st
I had heard much of the good order of Knutsford House of Correction and on my inspection of it this day (through the kindness of Revd. Michell). I was in no way disappointed.
J.P. and Dep. Lieutenant from Suffolk

1859 April 4th
Visited the gaol and went through the Weaving Dept. which is much improved by the introduction of a winding machine – the management of the gaol throughout is very satisfactory.

1875 Sunday April 4th
Attended service in the Chapel and was pleased to see the order and manner in which it was conducted.

1877 September 28th
Accompanied Sir Edmund Du Cane and Admiral Hornby through the gaol on the occasion of their inspection of the building and arrangements as Government Commissioners.

Sometimes the comments were formal variations on the theme that all was well: "Visited the prison and was highly pleased", "Visited the prison and found all in good order", "Visited the prison and found all right".

When the Magistrates took to visiting after their regular meeting they completed the book by writing "Visited the Prison" and all present signed.

1915 September 22nd
Visited the Prison. (This is the last entry)

Rules for The House of Correction, dated July 13th 1824 (Extracts). As required by Statute 4 Geo. 4 Cap 64

The Keepers Journal directed to be kept by the above mentioned Rules shall contain a register of the following particulars relating to each prisoner committed to his charge. viz the name, age, stature, complexion, colour of hair, trade or profession and place of abode, by whom committed, for what offence and upon what sentence. To which shall be added the time and manner of the prisoner's discharge.

The same journal shall state the name and offence of every prisoner who shall conduct himself or herself in the prison and the nature, date and term of his or her punishment for such offence and by whose authority that punishment was inflicted. It shall also state the names of such prisoners as shall observe these rules, regularly attend public worship, show extraordinary industry and behave in a peaceable and orderly manner to the intent that rewards may be applied accordingly to such report and such journal shall contain a general account of all the transactions in the prison.

All the prisoners under sentence… provided they receive the County allowance and prisoners before trial working with their own consent, shall unless prevented by sickness be employed for so many hours in each day (except on Sundays, Christmas Day, Good Friday and Days of Fasting and Thanksgiving) as the daylight in the different seasons of the year will admit not exceeding ten hours in the whole, exclusive of half an hour to be allowed for Breakfast, one hour for Dinner and half an hour for Supper. No prisoner shall be placed together on account of employment who would otherwise be kept separate (except by permission of a Visiting Magistrate).

The prayers directed by the rules contained in the above mentioned Act of Parliament shall be read twice in the week by the Chaplain and every other morning (except such days whereon Divine service is performed in the chapel) by him or by such other person as the Visiting Magistrates shall from time to time direct.

Scales and weights legally stamped shall be furnished to the Keeper at the expense of the County for the free use of all the prisoners between the hours of twelve and one each day for the weighing of any articles supplied to them.

The Keeper or some one appointed by him shall also examine all letters to or from any of the prisoners and shall not forward or deliver any letter which shall contain any improper matter but shall forth with shew the same to the Chaplain or one of the Visiting Magistrates for his opinion and advice thereon and in case of such letters being addressed to any prisoner shall without delay send for such prisoner and read to him or her the unacceptable part of such letter and in the case of letters coming from any prisoner shall without delay send such prisoner and state to him or her the objection to such letter that such prisoner may if he or she shall think fit write another letter in lieu thereof. There shall be no unnecessary delay in forwarding letters to or from any prisoner and the Keeper shall allow all letters to pass between prisoners for trial and their attornies which shall contain only matter relevant to their offences.

The prisoners own cloaths shall be cleaned and stoved, ticketed and laid up to be worn again on his or her trial or discharge and every prisoner committed for Felony or Misdemeanant shall on his or her admission into the prison and previously also to his or her discharge be cleansed and washed in the bath.

No prisoner after being locked up shall sing shout or make a noise in the cells or rooms.

Clean straw shall be provided for all the beds in the prison at least once in six months if in constant use or oftener if found necessary.

Each shall be supplied by the Keeper at the expense of the County with a chamberpot, a canvas straw bed, a blanket and

RULES FOR THE HOUSE OF CORRECTION, 1824

a rug and sheet of linen when thought necessary by the Visiting Magistrates and a mop-broom and bucket and wash bowl shall be also provided for each Day room.

These rules together with the other rules before referred to shall be read in the Chapel by the Keeper the first Sunday in every quarter immediately after Divine service in lieu of the sermon and shall be printed on strong paper and posted up in the respective wards and other conspicuous parts of the gaol so that every prisoner may have access thereto.

Chaplain. The Chaplain shall on every Sunday, Christmas Day and Good Friday perform Divine service according to the form of the Church of England and preach a sermon at morning and evening service. Morning service shall begin at half past ten o'clock and evening service at half past two and in addition to the duties required of him by the said Act he shall superintend such schools as may be established therein for the instruction of prisoners in reading and writing and make a report to the Visiting Magistrates of the progress the scholars may make.

Surgeon shall visit the prison twice at least in every week and oftener if necessary and shall see every prisoner confined therein and shall report to every General or Quarter Sessions the condition of the prison and the state of health of prisoners under his care.

Matron shall constantly reside in the prison.

She shall search every female prisoner on her admission into the prison and also any female visitant whom the Keeper may think proper to have examined.

She shall keep a regular journal and account of the conduct of the female prisoners and report to the keeper from time to time any particular instances of good behaviour or idle or refractory conduct amongst them.

She shall always attend Divine service with the female prisoners.

She shall keep an account of the female prisoners' earnings and shall be allowed 1/5th part of the clear profit thereof beyond which and her salary she shall not receive any fee or gratuity from any person or any account whatsoever.

Chester Record Office ref QAB 9/2

Rules for Misdemeanants in The House of Correction 1840

The Keeper. He shall enter into Bond in £400 for the due execution of his office and observance of the Rules. He shall not be concerned in any occupation of Trade whatsoever and shall not absent himself from the prison for a night without permission. He shall as may be practicable visit every ward and see every prisoner and inspect every cell once at least in every twenty four hours. He shall report daily to the Surgeon all complaints of sickness made by prisoners. He shall report to the Chaplain the prisoners absence from Divine service, with the cause that the Chaplain may visit them if necessary. He shall examine all articles supplied to the prison and if any shall be found of bad quality or not according to contract he shall return them and report it in his journal

The Chaplain. He shall be a person licensed by the Bishop of the Diocese and shall not hold any benefice with care of souls or any curacy. He shall administer the Holy Sacrament of the Lord's Supper to such prisoners as shall be desirious and as he may deem to be in a proper state of mind at least four times a year. He shall read prayers selected from the Liturgy of the Church of England every morning at nine o'clock. He shall frequently visit every room and cell in the prison occupied by prisoners and shall visit every prisoner in the Hospital or in Solitary Confinement daily. He shall frequently see and converse with the prisoners alone and inquire into the state of mind of each individual. He shall visit those absent from worship, instruct the prisoners in their moral duties, give spiritual advice and religious consolation and attend particularly to any prisoner who may desire his assistance.

The Surgeon. Shall be a member of one of the Royal Colleges of Surgeons. He shall examine every prisoner brought in and twice each week see every prisoner in the prison in his or her cell. He shall attend whenever a prisoner undergoes corporal punishment and shall have power to lessen the degree of punishment when he may think the health and strength of the prisoner requires it. He shall if he believes the mind or body of any prisoner is materially affected by the discipline, treatment or diet of the prison report the same in writing to the Keeper and state the changes that he wishes to be made. He shall keep a journal in the prison in which he shall enter in the English language day by day an account of the state of every sick prisoner, the name of his or her disease, a description of the medicines or diet or any other treatment which he may order for such prisoner, the date of every attendance.

Punishment. The Keeper has power to hear all complaints as to disobedience of the Rules of the prison. Assaults by one prisoner upon another when no dangerous wounds or bruise is given – Profane cursing or swearing – any indecent behaviour – any irreverent behaviour in chapel – absence from chapel without leave and idleness or negligence in work – and to punish the offender by close confinement in the refractory or solitary cells and by keeping him upon bread and water only for any term not exceeding three days.

General Rules. No convicted prisoner shall be allowed to send or receive a letter oftener than once in three months. No tap shall be kept in the prison and no prisoner shall be allowed to have any wine, ale, beer, porter or any other fermented liquor or any tobacco unless ordered by the Surgeon. No pigs, fowls or dogs shall be kept within the prison walls except dogs for security.

Clothing for Females. The following wearing apparel shall be provided for prisoners at the cost of the County. A cotton Cap. A cotton Bedgown. Two wollen Petticoates. Two cotton Chemises and a pair of Clogs.

REFERENCES

Labour for Females. The labour shall consist of the washing of articles belonging to the prison – of repairing articles of prison dress and such other work as shall from time to time be provided by the Keeper.

Diet for Females. The Diet shall be the same as herein before stated with respect to Male prisoners and an allowance of one pint of new milk per day shall be made for each child brought into the prison with the mother but no child whose age exceeds twelve months shall be received with the mother.

Chester Record Office ref QAB 9/3

KNUTSFORD PRISON – THE INSIDE STORY

A Famous Knutsford Hotel

In Knutsford's fair town there are first class hotels
Where they give board and lodging for all the big swells
They've all blinds on the windows and bolts on the doors
And beautiful carpet laid down on the floors.

But the grandest of all and now in full swing
Is the fine looking hostel controlled by the king.
I was in it myself and am able to tell
There's no digs in Europe to equal Knutsford Hotel.

I was met at the first by a porter and bus
They drove me along wid a great deal of fuss.
We went right in the town like a viceroy in state
And never drew rein 'till we stopped at the gate.

I was sint in a room took down my name
They axed my address and the reason I came,
When I'd answered the questions, the clerk rang a bell
And a bath I indulged in at Knutsford Hotel.

When I'd got thro' the bath my blood was quite froze
An attendant brought in a fine new suit of clothes
The finish was great and the pattern quite grand
And over them all was a beautiful band.

Then dinner was served 'twas a glorious feast.
There must have been five or six courses at least.
Och' the brandy and whiskey, they made my head swell;
I was drunk as a lord at Knutsford Hotel.

I wint for a walk every day, round the grounds.
But the guests as ye know, have to kape within bounds.
When I axed for my 'dudeen' (for I wanted a smoke)
Says the boss there quite stiffly 'D' ye think it a joke'.

A FAMOUS KNUTSFORD HOTEL

I'm sorry says I ye've taken me so
Maybe for a brandy and water ye'll go.
Says he 'bread and water might do you as well'
And I got them all free at the self same hotel

I spent there some months – how the time seemed to go.
There kindness was great, ~~faith~~ they treated me so.
I'd light and attendance, and everything free
Not to mention the extras and afternoon tea.

And when the day came from them I'd to part
I nearly dropped dead with a sigh in my heart
But with kindness so great, the truth I must tell
I'll stay at the 'George' ~~or 'Angel'~~ when I want a hotel.

An undated skit on the prison.
Was to be sung to the tune 'Mountains of Mourne'
(Seen at an exhibition about the prison at Knutsford Heritage Centre)

References

1. James Neild "State of the Prisons in England Scotland and Wales" 1812 pg 394.
2. QAB9/1.
3. QAB8/4181/1.
4. Asa Briggs "The Age of Improvement" Longman 1959 pg 295.
5. 1843 QAB9/5.
6. 1843 QAB9/5.
7. 1843 Report of The Inspector of Prisons QAB 9/5.
8. Parliamentary Papers 1843 XL1 11.
9. Parliamentary Papers 1843 XL1 11.
10. 1843 QAB 9/5.
11. Parliamentary Papers 1843 XL111.
12. October 1836 QAB 8/1/1.
13. March 1843 QAB8/1/2.
14. July 1st 1844 QAB 8/1/2.
15. February 20th 1835 QAB8/4181/1.
16. June 25th 1853 QAB8/1/3.
17. February 22nd 1839 QAB 8/1/1.
18. February 22nd 1839 QAB8/1/1.
19. Second Report of Inspectors of Prisons.
20. October 11th 1851 QAB8/1/3.
21. October 11th 1851 QAB8/1/3.
22. January 1877 *QAB8/1/5*.
23. QAB/8/4181/1.
24. QAB/8/4181/1.
25. QAB/8/1/2.
26. QAB 8/4181/1.
27. 1847 Thirteenth Report of Inspectors of Prisons.
28. QAB/8/1.
29. QAB/8/1.
30. QAB/8/4181/1.
31. May 11th 1844 QAB/8/1/2.
32. October 13th 1832 QAB 8/4181/1.

REFERENCES

33. December 28th 1850 QAB8/1/3.
34. March 19th 1844 QAB8/1/2.
35. 1856 QAB8/1/3.
36. December 11th 1852 QAB8/1/3.
37. May 29th 1835 QAB8/4181/1.
38. May 29th 1835 QAB8/4181/1.
39. March 17th 1843 QAB8/1/2
40. June 12th 1847 QAB8/1/2.
41. Second Report of Inspectors of Prisons pg 24ff 1837.
42. October 12th 1844 QAB1/2.
43. George Heaton "The Clergyman in the Gaol: An Essay on Prison Discipline" London 1847 pg 64.
44. Thirteenth Report of Inspectors of Prisons 1847 pg.30ff
45. April 4th 1846 QAB1/3.
46. Fourth Report of Inspectors of Prisons 1839.
47. Fourth Report of Inspectors of Prisons 1839.
48. Thirteenth Report of Inspectors of Prisons 1847.
49. August 11th 1849 QAB8/1/3.
50. April 11th 1844 QAB1/2.
51. January 3rd 1852 QAB8/1/3.
52. September 24th 1853 QAB8/1/3.
53. December 29th 1866 QAB8/1/4.
54. June 1875 QAB8/1/5.
55. May 1868 QAB8/1/4.
56. September 4th 1852 QAB8/1/3.
57. June 1861 QAB8/1/3.
58. Select Committee on Gaols and Houses of Correction 1835 pg 24.
59. January 20th 1847 QAB8/1/2.
60. 1852 QAB8/1/3.
61. January 2nd 1846 QAB8/1/2.
62. November 1847 QAB8/1/2.
63. April 1st 1876
64. December 2nd 1881
65. June 2nd 1882
66. Departmental Committee on Instruction of Prisoners

1896 pg 26f
67. Departmental Committee on Instruction of Prisoners 1896 XIII
68. July 1898 QAB8/5/6.
69. 1905 QAB8/5/8.
70. QAB8/5/7.
71. January 31st 1904 QAB8/5/5.
72. 1904 QAB8/5/9.
73. January 16th 1908 QAB5/10. -

The records consulted at The Cheshire Records in Chester can be found under:

Quarter Sessions : Administration: Buildings. Gaol and Sessions House at Knutsford QAB8.

Index

A

Akers-Douglas, Mr. 71
Algoa Bay 28
American System 24
Ammunition Store 54
Andrews, Captain (Church Army) 76
Anti-Corn Law League 6
Archbishop of Canterbury 7
Army Council 75, 77
Attornies, letters to 84
Australia, transportation 49

B

Basket Making 17
Bateson, Mr 5
Bath 84
Beds 84
Bevan, Thomas 66
Bexton Road 77
Billington (Hangman) 67
Birkenhead 67
Birmingham, Winson Green Gaol 72, 73
Bishop of Chester 31
Boon, Mary 33
Borstal System 76
Bramall, Thomas 9
Brannon-Lee, - 80
Bread manufacture 64
Brown, John 40
Brown, Mary 33, 50
Browne, Revd. William Robert 11, 23, 29
Burgess, Mr Edward 8, 10, 13, 20, 25, 29
Burke, Mary 57

C

Caldecott, Mr. 71

Cannon, A. A. 77
Carnarvon, Lord A7, 52
Cat 72, 74
Chapel 30
Chaplain 8, 10, 11, 12, 23, 24, 59, 64, 65, 67, 70, 76, 83, 84, 85, 87
    Clerk to 26
    Salary 26
Chartists 6, 8, 13, 29, 36, 46
Chelford 47
Cheshire and Chester Archives and Local Studies A8, 75
Cheshire Yeomanry 54
Chester Castle 65
Chester Chronicle, The 3
Chester Prison 1, 6, 46, 47, 55, 65
Children 27, 28, 42, 89
Christian Knowledge Society 27
Christmas, Mr 13, 15, 20, 25, 79
Church Army, The 76
Clay, John 14, 25
Clerk to the Chaplin 26
Clothing 84, 88
Commission of Assize, Chester 1842 7
Congleton 7, 28
Connor, Captain 13
Constable of Chester Castle 2
Constables 50
Corporal Punishment 71, 72, 73
Countryman's Rambler, The 5
County 2, 5, 13, 22, 84
County Court debtors 16
Court of Quarter Sessions 12
Crank 17, 19, 56
Crewe 66
Cubbit, Wlliam 18

D

Daily Chronicle, The 64
Dalton, Joseph 20

Davenport, Mr 78, 79, 80
Davis, George 66
Davis, Robert 66
Deane 36
Deane, Dr Richard T 8, 9, 32, 33
Deaths 44, 56
Departmental Committee of Enquiry into the Execution of the Death Penalty 66
Departmental Committee on Education 1896 64
Detention Barracks 77
Diet 9, 34, 51, 56, 63, 81, 89
Dipping, John 57
Discipline 19
Disinfection 32, 84
Du Cane, Sir Edmund 60, 64, 82
Dunscom, Thomas MP 8

E

Egerton, Lord 71, 78, 79
Employment 83
Evangelicals 24
Executioner 66
Executions 65
Exeter House of Correction 3

F

Female Prisoners 16, 33, 88
    Children 89
    Diet 89
    Labour 89
Fenians 57, 58
Fennell, Dr. Theodore 32, 70
Fever 36
Fire, In the Prison 1853 54
Food 34. See Diet
Fowles, Mr 30
France, Inspector General of Prisons 23

G

Gallop, Mr George 13, 15, 20, 22, 34, 51, 60, 81
Gaol Distemper Act 1777 32
Gatley, John 20
Gillman 4
Gladstone, Hubert 64
Gloucester Prison 79
Govan, William 79
Governor 8, 10, 11, 12, 17, 19, 22, 26, 55, 56, 76, 77, 80, 81, 85, 87
    Deputy Governor 22
    House 30, 47, 48
Graham, John 69
Graham, Sir James 8, 10, 36
Graham's Dietary 52
Grand Jury Room 2
Grey Committee 52
Guardian, The 66, 67

H

Habeas Corpus 57
Habitual Criminals Act 1869 57
Hancocks, William Alfred 66
Hard Labour 74, 79
Hardy, John 50
Harris, Dr. 69
Hartigan, Edward 67
Heap, William 4, 5
Henry, Dr. 32
High Sheriff of the County 66
Hills-Johnes G.C.B., V.C., Lt. General J. 72
Hodson, - 80
Holford 17
Holford Committee 1810 11, 29
Holland, Frank 73

Home Office 56, 57, 70, 71, 73
Home Secretary 8, 11, 13, 46, 57, 65, 67, 70, 73, 74
Hornby, Admiral 60, 82
House of Correction 2
Howard, John A7, 23, 32, 77
Hudson, Mr 5, 79

I

Inspector General of Prisons in France 23
Irons 79

J

Jarvis, Mary 33, 50
Jebb, Major 16
Joynson, Mr. R. H. 72, 76
Juveniles 27, 28, 40, 42, 49, 50

K

Keeper. See Governor
Keepers Journal 83
Knutsford Historical Association A8, 39, 41, 48, 62, 65
Knutsford Parish Church 66

L

Labour for Females 89
Lamb, William 78
le Breton, Thomas 14
Legh, Mr George 5, 78, 81
Leicester Gaol 3
Leigh, Egerton 5, 49, 79, 80
Lenham, John 70
Letters 84
Lewes Prison 77
Lewis, Mr Hornby 66
Liverpool Prison 70, 73, 77

London and North West Railway 48
Lynch, Fr. Hugh 58

M

Macclesfield 7, 28
   Workhouse 51
Magistrates 2, 9, 10, 11, 14, 15, 16, 17, 18, 19, 20, 32, 33, 39, 40, 47, 49, 50, 51, 53, 54, 56, 57, 58, 60, 63, 69, 70, 72, 74, 78, 83, 84
Mainwaring, Harry 8, 80, 81
Mainwaring, Sir Henry 5, 78
Manchester 32
   City Gaol 59, 77
   New Bailey 32
Manchester Times, The 6
Matron 29, 38, 79, 85
McGill, Owen 66
Mellor, Thomas 78
Mellor, William 30
Merriman, Dr. Charles 32
Middlewich House of Correction 1, 2
Millbank Penitentiary, London 25, 33, 47
Minutes of the Visiting Magistrates 14
Mitchell, Revd. Charles 23, 28, 30, 81
Moneypenny, George 3, 4

N

Neild, James 1, 2
Nelson, Major 13

O

O'Reilly, Fr. 58
Oakley, William 52
Over 67

P

Parker, Sir Thomas 5

Peel, Sir John A7
Pennethorn, Captain 13, 69
Peterloo 7
Petworth Prison 3
Philanthropic Farm School 28
Philipps, James 67
Phillips, John 34
Photography 57
Plug Riots 7
Porter, The 38
Potts, James 53
Powell, Joseph 22
Poynton 7
Preston Goal 14, 17, 25, 54
Price, Charlotte 29
Prison Act 1824 A7, 77
Prison Act 1865 A7, 52, 57
Prison Commission A8, 60, 61, 66, 71, 73
Prison Commissioners 60, 64, 69
Prison Inspectors A7, 8, 10, 11, 15, 16, 20, 25, 26, 27, 38, 54, 56, 60
Prison Ministers Act 1863 58
Prison Officers 38, 54, 74
Prison Service College A8
Prisoners Aid Grants 61
Prisons Act 1877 60
Prisons Bill 1876 60
Punishment 20, 33, 36, 42, 46, 64, 72, 79, 83, 88

Q

Quarter Sessions 12, 37, 42, 85
Queen Victoria 7

R

Railway 47
Randle, Mr. 78
Roche, Fr. 76

Roman Catholic priests 58, 76
Roulby, Revd. John 23
Ruggles-Brise, Mr. 73
Rules for The House of Correction 83
Runcorn 4
Russell, Mr Charles 77
Russell, Revd. Whitworth 25

S

Salt Union, The 67
Sanitation 17, 84
Scaffold 65
Scales and weights 84
Schoolmaster 22, 26, 38, 64
Screw 40
Scurvy 36
Select Committee of the House of Lords 1835 27
Separate System 15, 24, 81
Sessions House 2, 61, 62, 65
Shot drill 55, 57
Silent System 14, 25
Slack, Miss 26
Smith, Sidney 17
Solitary Confinement 79, 88
Spenser, John 74
Spicer, Felix 66
St Peter's Field, Manchester 7
Stafford Prison 18, 52, 77
Stanley Road 77
Stanley Terrace 39
Stanley, Sir John 5
Stephen, - 80
Stephens, Revd. Joseph Rayner 6
Stockport 28
    Workhouse 51
Supervisor of Prison Building 16
Surgeon 8, 10, 20, 32, 56, 80, 85, 87
    Salary 26
Sutcliffe, Dr. William 32

T

Talbot-Price, Captain RN 13, 60
Tanner, Edward 33
Taskmaster 10, 38, 80
Taunton Gaol 52
Toft Road 77
Townshend, Mr. 81
Trafford, Mr. 78, 79
Transportation 46, 47, 50, 53
Treadmill 8, 18, 19, 56, 79
Truss, Revd. William 23, 59, 64, 76
Turner, Edward 11
Turner, Richard 50
Turnkeys 33, 38, 78

U

Uniform 39, 41, 54, 61

V

Van Dieman's Land 47, 49
Vannett, Revd. Peter 23, 24, 26, 27
Visiting Committee 61, 71, 72, 73, 74, 76, 77
Visiting Justices 5, 11, 12, 19, 22, 61

W

Wakefield prison 15, 25
Walpole, Horatio 65
Warders 38
Watchman 38
Weaving 81
Whitby, John 57
White, John 79
Whitely, Jock 79
Wibraham, Mr. 78
Williams, Captain 7, 17
Wincham 4
Winchester Gaol 3
Winson Green Gaol, Birmingham 72, 73
Winstanley, Miss 76
Woods, Mr 19
Woolpicking 18, 50
Work 17, 19
Workhouse 51
   Act 1834 52
Wright, Miss 76
Wright, Mr 29
Wright, William 8

Y

York Prison 18

Léonie Press local books include:

MEMORIES OF A CHESHIRE CHILDHOOD – MEMORIAL EDITION
Lenna Bickerton (ISBN 978-1-901253-13-9) £4.99

"WE'LL GATHER LILACS..."
Lenna Bickerton (ISBN 978-1-901253-21-4) £5.99

DIESEL TAFF
From 'The Barracks' to Tripoli
Austin Hughes (ISBN 978-1-901253-14-6) £8.99

A NUN'S GRAVE
A novel set in the Vale Royal of England
Alan K Leicester (ISBN 978-1-901253-08-5) £7.99

NELLIE'S STORY
A Life of Service
Elizabeth Ellen Osborne (ISBN 978-1-901253-15-3) £5.99

THE WAY WE WERE
Omnibus edition incorporating Over My Shoulder and Another's War
Les Cooper (ISBN 978-1-901253-07-8) £7.99

A HOUSE WITH SPIRIT
A Dedication to Marbury Hall
Jackie Hamlett and Christine Hamlett (ISBN 978-1-901253-19-1) £8.99

WOOLLYBACK
Alan Fleet (ISBN 978-1-901253-18-4) £8.99

A WHIFF OF FRESH AIR (plus CD)
A collection of humorous Cheshire monologues
Margaret Dignum (ISBN 978-1-901253-20-7) £9.99

MID-CHESHIRE MEMORIES – VOLUME 1
The Horseman and his Family; The Apprentice Mechanic's Tale; The Apprentice Fitter's Tale; The Fireman's Tale of the End of Steam
E E Osborne, G Mellor P Buckley and B Fisher
(ISBN 978-1-901253-28-3) £8.99

From Léonie Press, 13 Vale Rd, Hartford, Northwich, Cheshire CW8 1PL.   Website: www.leoniepress.com